SEATBELTS
&VITAMINS

A Primer For Navigating the Coming Days

Marlow C. Hunter

Paperback ISBN: 978-1-7353701-0-1
Ebook ISBN: 978-1-7353701-1-8

REL046000   RELIGION / Christianity / Church of Jesus Christ of Latter-day Saints

Cover designed by Shaun McMurdie
Typeset by Kaitlin Barwick
Edited by Valene Wood and Kaitlin Barwick
Produced by Emily Chambers

For more information, please visit:
www.AuthorMarlowCHunter.com

Contents

Preface v

Chapter 1: Seatbelts & Vitamins 1

Chapter 2: His Yoke, Our Crosses—
Paradox of Burden and Blessing 10

Chapter 3: "I Will Turn Away Your Captivity" 19

Chapter 4: Less-Than-Divine Answers 30

Chapter 5: Grace: God's Gift to Change Us
from Fallen to Unfallen 41

Chapter 6: Rescuing 60

Chapter 7: Healing Physical and Spiritual Sickness ... 71

Chapter 8: "Believest thou the words which I shall speak?" ... 79

Chapter 9: Which Way Do We Face? 88

Chapter 10: Prayer and Gifts of the Spirit 100

Chapter 11: Covenants and Abrahamic Tests 107

Chapter 12: Commandments and Service 120

Chapter 13: "Hope" 132

Chapter 14: Scriptures = Super Vitamins 146

Chapter 15: Conclusion 161

Bibliography 169
About the Author 174

Preface

The genesis of this literary effort was embodied in a long thought-out decision to retire from my career of forty-five years as a certified public accountant (CPA—USA). Lest there be any confusion or misunderstanding as to my motivations for reaching that conclusion, I was not, as happens to many people, "burned out" or "disenchanted with" the day-to-day demands of providing professional accounting, auditing, and tax services to my clientele. It was simply, as many colleagues told me when responding to my inquiry as to why they had retired when they did, "You will know when it is time." My time arrived in January 2020. Most things went pretty much as I expected, including the withdrawal pains from a world defined by deadlines. One of the standing jokes in my profession is, "Did you survive April 15?" (the due date for personal income tax returns in the USA). My usual reply was, "Well, for me, every month has a fifteenth." My work-life was generally dictated by monthly deadlines—which was fine with me since it spaced out my workload over the entire year. Retirement status found me needing an entirely new time-usage model. No longer driven by deadlines, I found myself trying to construct a new model of what my daily life would consist.

Anxiety over discovering what I would do to fill my newly found available time gradually increased. I became more and more unsettled and struggled to find a new daily routine. Surprisingly, the answer emerged out of the preparation activities I undertake each week to magnify my church responsibility. For the past fifteen years, I have had the privilege of conducting a weekly adult gospel study session that is affectionately known as "Gospel Doctrine on Steroids." In December 2019, we completed a stimulating and fascinating three-year deep-dive into the Book of Mormon, and I asked the participants who attend our sessions where they wanted to go next. After some discussion and collaborative deliberation, a consensus was reached. We mutually determined that we would focus our educational experience on the book of Abraham, a topic we had previously studied in 2008. This decision turned out to be fortuitous.

As I began researching various materials, books, and journals, I stumbled across a new website developed by Brigham Young University (BYU) called "Pearl of Great Price Central," which is a spin-off from the widely popular and successful "Book of Mormon Central" website. Upon searching through the resources assembled on this invaluable site, I noticed that the initial efforts were centered, of all possible topics, on the book of Abraham. One of the extremely helpful resources on the site is a new study edition of the Pearl of Great Price, which I downloaded and proceeded to read with great interest. Once again, a phenomenon familiar to and no doubt experienced by you, the reader, occurred as I was reading; a particular portion of Abraham 1:18, "I will lead thee by my hand," lit up like a neon sign. Who put that phrase there? Surely, that had not been there the last time I studied the book of Abraham—I had not even highlighted or underlined these words in prior readings of the Book of Abraham. Yet that day, they hit me with great power and understanding. I was to let the Lord lead me by *His* hand. The anxiety and unsettled feelings in my heart and mind quickly dissipated. I was to write a second book. Hence, we have what follows.

Soon thereafter, while I was engaged in preparing PowerPoint materials for the study sessions on Abraham, I found myself reviewing past lessons, as I often do to ensure continuity of thought. I encountered a quote from President Ezra Taft Benson that confirmed that the impression I had received from reading in the book of Abraham was an answer to prayer. President Benson said, "Certain blessings are to be found only in the scriptures."[1] My task now was to trust that my Heavenly Father would lead me by His hand as I began to focus my study of His revealed word given through ancient and modern prophets to assemble material to include in this written endeavor. I connected what had been revealed to me with another of my favorite verses from Abraham: "Thy servant has sought thee earnestly; *now I have found thee . . . I will do well to hearken unto thy voice*" (Abraham 2:12–13; emphasis added). With these words, I was now totally confident that writing a second book was the direction I should go.

Having described the background and circumstances that resulted in the writing of this book, I want to express warmest greetings of love, friendship, and fellowship to all members of the Church and former members of the Church who might read what I have assembled herein. My objective is to cause two things to happen in readers' lives.

First, I want each of you to come to a greater realization that trusting our Father in Heaven and His eternal plan of happiness is the bedrock of the fulness of the gospel as taught by the prophets, seers, and revelators in The Church of Jesus Christ of Latter-day Saints. It has been my experience as a priesthood leader over the years that the erosion of such trust is the bottom-line explanation as to why a person leaves the Church. The opposite is true—a person who maintains an unwavering trust in God the Father and His plan finds himself or herself safely on the covenant path and moving forward to the tree of life. I am sure you noticed that I used the word *trust* in lieu of faith. I fear that many have begun to or have stopped trusting God and the promises made to the fathers (such as Abraham, Isaac, and Jacob), one of which is that He will deliver us. (See, for example, Psalms 54:7; 81:7; 107:6; 116:8; Isaiah 46:4; Daniel 3:17 & 29; Joel 2:32.)

Second, I want each reader to increase his or her *faith* in Jesus Christ and His atoning sacrifice for everyone who has lived on this earth, those who are now living on the face of the earth, and those who will yet receive their physical bodies and come to live on this earth prior to the Millennium. Once we begin not trusting God the Father, faith in His Only Begotten Son starts disintegrating. Only by having unmovable trust in God and unshakable faith in Jesus Christ will we be willing and able to let God guide us by His hand along the covenant path to eternal happiness.

As discussed in the ensuing chapter, we have been counseled that the days ahead are going to be difficult both for the Church as an institution and for us as individual members. We are undoubtedly going to be challenged to trust God as we proclaim and demonstrate our faith in Jesus Christ. We will need seatbelts solidly anchored to an unyielding trust in God and vitamins to give us the strength and endurance to endure as true disciples of Christ. Only then will we be able to navigate the coming days.

Note

1. Ezra Taft Benson, "The Power of the Word," *Ensign*, May 1986.

Chapter 1
Seatbelts & Vitamins

I wish to understand the wonders of Thy hand,
for all the blessings that are mine arise from Thy design.
(Sabbath Day Jewish Prayer)

In a video presentation during his South American tour following the October 2018 General Conference, President Russell M. Nelson lovingly warned us: "Wait till next year. And then the next year. Eat your vitamin pills. Get your rest. It's going to be exciting."[1] And in 2004, Elder Neal A. Maxwell said, "I don't know what lies ahead of you . . . but my advice would be to fasten your seatbelts and hold on firmly to your principles!"[2] These prophetic words suggest that many exciting events are going to happen at a faster pace as the Lord continues the process of restoring the fulness of the gospel of Jesus Christ to prepare His people for the Second Coming and to overcome Satan's last-ditch efforts to destroy God's work of "bring[ing] to pass the immortality and eternal life of man" (Moses 1:39).

As I pondered the images of seatbelts and vitamins, I concluded that seatbelts are associated with being anchored to the unmovable and indestructible foundation of trusting God the Father, His plan, and His promise to deliver us. Vitamins are supplements that continually ratify our faith in Jesus Christ and His atoning sacrifice by which God the Father extends grace to all who willingly choose to accept such an immeasurable gift. Seatbelts and vitamins will enable us in both our short- and long-term gospel living to withstand all the calamities that will be associated with and usher in the Millennium.

Seatbelts

Over the past fifteen years, I have had the privilege of visiting some sixty countries around this beautiful planet where we are so blessed to live as we experience mortality and prepare for immortality. During these travels, I have been on airplanes, boats, trains, cars, buses, and more, all of which had some form of seatbelt which was intended for safety purposes. It occurs to me that there are seatbelts to be found in the scriptures and the words of our living prophets by which, if prayerfully studied and then incorporated into our daily lives by way of the guidance of the Holy Ghost, we can maintain unfailing trust in God, His plan, and His promise of deliverance. We then can faithfully traverse the covenant path to the tree of life safely and successfully, regardless of the worldly calamities going on around us. Therefore, I have assembled ideas and suggestions that I hope will serve you as "seatbelts and vitamins," providing safety and strength to get back on and stay on the covenant path.

It seems to me that if we are to "buckle up," then we should be checking to see that our seatbelt is in top working condition and that it is properly attached to the correct vehicle. As I continued pondering the imagery of seatbelts, reflecting what the near-term future of our journey along the covenant path might look like, it occurred to me that there must be a significant connection to President Nelson's invitation to revisit and study in depth the four major events inaugurating the advent of the Restoration—namely, the First Vision, the coming forth of the Book of Mormon, the bestowal of priesthood authority and restoring the ordinance of baptism, and lastly the organization of the Church in 1830.[3]

Seatbelts provide safety and protection only if anchored to the sure foundation that we call truth as embodied in the Church. That sure foundation was described by President Joseph Fielding Smith in a statement made at the October 1952 General Conference:

> So far as the philosophy and wisdom of the world are concerned, they mean nothing unless they conform to the revealed word of God. Any doctrine, whether it comes in the name of religion, science, philosophy, or whatever it may be, if it is in conflict with the revealed word of the Lord, will fail. It may appear plausible.

It may be put before you in language that appeals and which you may not be able to answer. It may appear to be established by evidence that you cannot controvert. . . . You will find that every doctrine, every principle, no matter how universally believed, if it is not in accord with the divine word of the Lord to his servants, will perish. Nor is it necessary for us to try to stretch the word of the Lord in a vain attempt to make it conform to these theories and teachings. The word of the Lord shall not pass away unfulfilled, but these false doctrines and theories will fail. Truth and only truth will remain when all else has perished.[4]

President Smith is giving us profound assurance that the doctrines of the gospel as revealed to His holy prophets are going to be in conflict with the prevailing philosophies and theories of scientific thoughts of the current and future days. He predicts that many people will fall victim to the enticing secularist notions of what life is all about and that there will be pressure put on the Church to conform doctrines to modern thinking about societal mores, cultural norms, and trending behaviors. We must tenaciously cling to true doctrines in the face of what are sure to be more Korihors, Sherems, and Nehors. Further, given the attractiveness of some of the world's messages, it will take having developed our ability to receive personal revelation to discern them as false and untrue.

Chocolate-Covered Vitamins

As a society, we have become extremely conscious of our well-being. We carefully monitor our dietary intake, we engage in a variety of exercise routines (walking, swimming, biking, aerobics, etc.), and we try to maintain consistent sleep habits. In the health arena particularly, vitamins are consumed daily (1) to replace vitamins no longer produced by the body, (2) to supplement vitamins still present in the body, (3) to provide essential resources to body systems, such as immune systems, and (4) for overall strength, just to name a few.

Now, just imagine if we could have "chocolate-covered" spiritual vitamins? It would be much easier to convince ourselves to eat them regularly. They would be sweet and satisfying and supplemental to our health!

Chocolate-covered vitamins are my images of spiritual vitamins, supplements to sustain us on our journey along the covenant path. Perhaps it would be apropos to begin with a little light-hearted humor before the heavy lifting. The following lines are from that renowned artisan of prose and poetry—"Anonymous."

Chocolate Is a Vegetable
a.k.a., The Creedal Code of a Confirmed Chocoholic

Beans are vegetables. Thus, chocolate being derived from beans is a vegetable.

Sugar is derived from either sugar cane or sugar beets. Both are plants, which places them in the vegetable category.

Taking it one step further, chocolate candy bars contain milk, which is a dairy product. So chocolate candy bars are a health food. Chocolate-covered raisins, cherries, orange slices, and strawberries all count as fruit, so eat as many as you want.

If you have melted chocolate all over your hands, you are eating it too slowly. The problem: How to get 2 pounds of chocolate home from the store in a hot car. The solution: eat it in the parking lot with the air conditioner on full blast.

Diet Tip: Eat a chocolate bar before each meal. It will take the edge of your appetite and you will eat less food. If calories are an issue, store your uneaten chocolate on top of the refrigerator. Calories are afraid of heights, and they will jump out of the chocolate to protect themselves. (We are testing this with other snack foods as well.)

Does consuming an equal amount of dark chocolate and white chocolate constitute a balanced diet? Don't they counteract each other? Chocolate has many preservatives. Preservatives make us look younger. Therefore, we should eat more chocolate. A nice box of chocolates can provide our total daily intake of calories in one place. Now, isn't that handy?

Put "eat chocolate" at the top of our list of things to accomplish today. That way, we will get at least one thing done. But if you can't eat all your chocolate, what's wrong with you?

So as a confirmed chocoholic, you can see that I am doomed! But there is an upside to my humor. Given the plethora of vitamins on the market (visit a health food or nutrition supplement store and one is quickly overwhelmed by the hundreds of vitamins available), we need to determine which ones are the most appropriate for us to be taking— clearly the chocolate-covered ones! Refreshing and rethinking the seminal restoration activities which occurred on that small farm in Western New York from 1820 to 1830 are clearly chocolate-covered vitamins necessary to successfully navigate our way along the covenant path.

If you will permit just one example from my efforts—I discovered a series of six podcasts produced by the Church discussing the events and circumstances leading up to Joseph's magnificent theophany. One of those podcasts is an excellent presentation about the Sacred Grove. Having had the opportunity several years ago to visit the Smith farm located on the outskirts of Palmyra, New York, I wondered why Joseph chose to go to the grove of trees across the road from their home. Why not climb a mountain to converse with the Lord like other prophets such as Moses and Abraham? Certainly, there are several suitable hills (Cumorah comes to mind) near the Smith home that are easily accessible and would have provided the necessary seclusion. Why the grove? Well, it turns out that his mother had gone over to the stand of trees across the road from the Smith home and called upon the Lord on more than one occasion with her questions.[5] She recounted to Joseph about where she had gone to commune with God. Thus, Lucy Mack Smith played an unsuspecting but key role in the seminal, sacred event. I can hear her lovingly saying to her son, "When you have a religious crisis, you go to the woods and pray to God." Joseph's crisis was seeking ratification that his trust in God to provide wisdom was not misplaced. And what wisdom (a.k.a., chocolate vitamin) was Joseph seeking? Which church taught the right way to be saved from sin?

I encountered the following quote presented during an Academic Symposium held in 2005 where the topic was "The Worlds of Joseph Smith." One of the presenters, Arun Joshi, a Hindu journalist from India, shared this provocative insight:

"The message of Joseph Smith is more relevant today than ever before."[6]

Mr. Joshi's conclusion is even more true in 2020. Those who are brushing aside or letting doubts creep into their thinking the prophetic calling of Joseph and his successors are dangerously traveling through life by not taking their spiritual vitamins. Aside from being sure my seatbelt was riveted to the proper framework of the covenant path vehicle—the gospel of Jesus Christ as taught by the restored Church of Jesus Christ—I discovered a wealth of chocolate-covered vitamins that supplemented my testimony of this profound event and added immeasurable significance to these important foundational events:

- No Christian denomination has ever canonized its founder's biographical narrative to the status of scripture.
- Rather than locating his authority in scripture, Joseph rooted his commission as a prophet, seer, and revelator in angelic visions, and based his authority to restore the primitive church on his priesthood ordination at the hands of heavenly personages who held keys of the kingdom of God.
- As the waves of the second Great Awakening washed over the "burned-out district," the settlers in western New York wanted to hear sacred words from God: "We would hear God speak."[7]
- Echoing the sentiments cited above, Ralph Waldo Emerson told the Harvard Divinity School faculty and student body in 1838:

  > "We need to hear from God again. . . . I look for the hour when that Supreme Beauty, which ravished the souls of Eastern men [and women], chiefly the Hebrews, and through their lips spoke oracles for all time, shall speak in the West also."[8]

- The glorious theophany, which occurred in "sacred time" on that spring day in 1820, wherein the divine injunction of "Hear Him" shattered centuries of heavenly silence, began a continuing outpouring of "sacred words" ever since.
- Joseph produced a wealth of sacred words consisting of the Book of Mormon, the Book of Commandments (later changed to the

Doctrine and Covenants), the Joseph Smith Translation of the Bible, and the books of Moses and Abraham.

- The Saints canonized these sacred words virtually as soon as they were in print, considering them to have the same, or in some cases greater, authority than biblical texts.
- Why did the Saints believe the Lord was speaking sacred words to them? A striking rhetorical feature of the revelations partly explains their persuasiveness—namely, the voice in the revelations comes through as purely God's voice. Furthermore, God's gift of agency comes to the foreground: the Saints could decide to believe or not—they were free to hearken (D&C 1:1) or to turn away.
- In addition to the multitude of sacred words, Joseph planted the seed of sacred places—for example, Zion, the New Jerusalem. Even though that seed had to be replanted in three different parts of the Lord's vineyard (Kirtland, Missouri, and Nauvoo), before being finally sowed in the good soil of the Salt Lake Valley.
- In contrast to the several ministers and others to whom Joseph related what he considered to be significant portions of his vision and who then mocked his "tale," Joseph's father replied, "Never be disobedient to the vision."
- Approximately one year prior to his martyrdom, Joseph wrote: "If I had not actually got into this work and been called of God, I would back out. But I cannot back out: I have no doubt of the truth [vision]."[9]
- Remembering is sacramental. Remembering is to the past, what faith is to the future. Remembering past covenants of the Lord is not just an exercise in historiography; it is a stipulation required in making and keeping sacred covenants. (See Mosiah 5:11–12 and D&C 20:77 and 79.)
- The Prophet relied not only on the Holy Bible to recover lost sacred words, but he also relied on the past to recover authority. If we had the opportunity to ask Joseph what he gained from the past, he would likely speak first of the restoration of divine keys from angelic beings that govern priesthood powers and the authority to perform eternally binding ordinances in the name of Jesus Christ according to the will of the Father.

- The resounding and overriding message of the First Vision demonstrates God's unbounded compassion and love for His children. Joseph recounts, "For many days, I could rejoice with great joy."[10] God comes to the aid of those in spiritual distress. He is anxious to forgive. Though we mortals are sinful, we are not cast off. God will respond to honest inquiries.

My humble attempts to do as President Nelson invited us to do—re-explore and rediscover the marvels of the four major pillars of the Restoration, which herald the ushering in of the dispensation of the fulness of times—has become a blessing of comfort and strength to move forward with confidence in the coming days.

Navigational Tools

I am convinced that the Lord will lead you (and me) by His hand along the covenant path to the tree of life. For those who have strayed from the covenant path, if we willingly choose to let Him, He will lead us back to that path. For those still on the path, our commitment to stay on the path will be reinforced as we also willingly allow God to lead us by the hand. We know that the future course along the path will be challenging, to say the least, which reminds me of a Maxwell-ism: "Following celestial road signs while in telestial traffic jams is not easy."[11] None of us should be surprised that we have been counseled to "buckle up" and "take our vitamins" in anticipation of what lies ahead on the covenant path.

When organizing ideas to be included herein, my initial thought was to have two sections following this introductory chapter, namely, (1) Seatbelts and (2) Vitamins. However, as I started preparing a list of which topics would best fit in which section, I became increasingly dissatisfied with my characterizations. Eventually, I concluded that the best solution was to let you, the reader, make that decision based on your individual circumstances and situations. I remind the reader that for purposes of this literary effort, seatbelts are those gospel principles that either regain or maintain trust in God the Father, His plan, and the assurance that He will deliver us. Vitamins are those gospel principles that lead to and increase faith in Jesus Christ and His atoning sacrifice that we might be gathered (see John 11:52; Ephesians 1:10; 2 Nephi 29:14; D&C 33:6) to receive our inheritance in the kingdom of heaven. We are so thankful for prophets who lead and guide us in these latter days. But perhaps more importantly, we are grateful for the blessing of being able to receive personal revelation that will guide us in our quest along the covenant path. My sincere desire is that many of the topics included herein will serve as blessings to you.

So buckle up them seatbelts!
Chow down some chocolate vitamins!
Let's enjoy the ride together!

Notes

1. Russell M. Nelson, in "Latter-day Saint Prophet, Wife and Apostle Share Insights of Global Ministry." Oct. 30, 2018, *newsroom.ChurchofJesusChrist.org*.
2. Neal A. Maxwell, "Remember How Merciful the Lord Hath Been," *Ensign*, May 2004.
3. Russell M. Nelson, "Closing Remarks," *Ensign*, November 2019.
4. Joseph Fielding Smith, in Conference Report, October 1952, 58–59.
5. See Jean B. Bingham, "United in Accomplishing God's Work," *Ensign*, May 2020.
6. Arun Joshi, "Mormon Ways of Family Life Can Resolve Conflicts in World," paper delivered at *Ideas for the 21st Century: The Worlds of Joseph Smith*, National Taiwan University, Taipei, Taiwan, August 27, 2005.
7. Orestes Brownson, 1836, as quoted in David F. Holland, "Anne Hutchinson to Horace Bushnell: A New Take on the New England Sequence," *The New England Quarterly* 78, no. 2 (June 2005): 194.
8. Ralph Waldo Emerson, "An Address Delivered before the Senior Class in Divinity College, Cambridge, Sunday Evening, 15 July 1838" in the Collected Works of Ralph Waldo Emerson, ed. Robert E. Spiller and Alfred E Ferguson (Cambridge, MA: Belknap Press of Harvard University Press, 1971, 1:92).
9. Joseph Smith, in *History of the Church*, 5:336 (April 6, 1843).
10. Joseph Smith, in *Histories, Volume 1: Joseph Smith Histories, 1832–1844*, 12–13.
11. Neal A. Maxwell, "Notwithstanding My Weakness," *Ensign*, November 1976.

Chapter 2

His Yoke, Our Crosses– Paradox of Burden and Blessing

Help me to walk with good companions,
To live with Hope in my heart,
and Eternity in my thoughts,
That I may lie down in peace,
and rise up wanting to do thy will.

(Jewish Prayer for Shabbat)

During the third year of His ministry, while visiting Perea (a region on the east side of the Jordan River north of where it flows into the Dead Sea; the place where John the Baptist had been preaching and baptizing), Jesus issued what might be considered as a "strange," "confusing," and "paradoxical" invitation to His disciples:

> Take *my yoke* upon you, and learn of me; for I am meek and lowly in heart . . . for *my yoke* is easy, and my burden is light. (Matthew 11:29–30; emphasis added)

The paradox emerges when the Savior declares while introducing the parables of the lost sheep, the lost coin, the prodigal son, and the unjust steward:

> Whoever does not *bear his own cross* and come after me is not able to be my disciple. (Luke 14:27, Wayment Translation; emphasis added)

Things get even more confusing when Jacob, brother of Nephi and high priest overseeing the temple, preaches the annual sermon of repentance required by the law of Moses on Yom Kippur (Day of Atonement, the holiest day in the Jewish year), and describes righteous saints of the Holy One of Israel as those "who have endured the *crosses of the world*" (2 Nephi 9:18; emphasis added). Apparently, there are two types of crosses—ones of our own making and ones that the world makes for us. These ancient images of a yoke and a cross need to be sorted out since many readers may not be familiar with them. This chapter will examine ways in which a yoke and a cross—images familiar to those living in the meridian of time—have application today. The following sections will address several key questions that will lead us to greater understanding and the desire to take upon ourselves His yoke coupled with our daily crosses. How does taking upon ourselves His yoke become one of the important ways in which we can "Hear him?" How do we manage both His yoke and our crosses?

Our Crosses

Life presses all kinds of burdens or crosses on each of us, some light but others heavy and relentless. Many of us struggle every day under burdens that vex our souls. These burdens can be emotionally or physically ponderous. They can be worrisome, oppressive, and exhausting. Sadly, they can continue for years.

In a general sense, we can identify three sources for our burdens. Some burdens are the natural product of the conditions of the fallen world we live in. Illness, physical disability, and many natural disasters occur from time to time through no fault of our own. We prepare for these risks, and we can sometimes predict their arrival, but in the natural pattern of life, we will all encounter some of these types of burdens.

Other burdens are imposed on us by the misconduct of others, whether intentional or unintentional. Abuse and addictions can make mortality anything but a heaven on earth for innocent family and friends. Incorrect traditions, repression, and crime scatter burdened victims along the pathways of life. Even less serious misdeeds such as gossip, unkindness, or lack of thoughtfulness can cause genuine suffering and unnecessary burdens.

Lastly, our own mistakes and shortcomings produce many of our problems and can place heavy crosses on our own shoulders. The most onerous cross we impose on ourselves is the burden of sin and transgression. We all have felt the shame, remorse, and pain that inevitably follow failure to keep the commandments and honor our covenants.

Regardless of our unique burdens, whether the consequence of natural conditions, the misconduct of others, or of our own mistakes and shortcomings, we must remember that such crosses are tailored to help us prepare to return to Heavenly Father. Burdens provide opportunities to practice virtues that contribute to eventual perfection. They invite us to

> yield to the enticings of the Holy Spirit and put off the natural man and become a saint through the Atonement of Christ the Lord; and becometh as a child, submissive, meek, humble, patient, full of love, willing to submit to all things which the Lord seeth fit to inflict upon us, even as a child doth submit to his father. (Mosiah 3:19)

Thus, crosses become blessings, though often such blessings are well disguised and may require time, effort, personal revelation, and faith to understand and accept.

Jesus declared, on the occasion of being in Caesarea Philippi with Peter, "If any man [or woman] will come after me, let him deny himself, and *take up his cross*, and follow me" (Matthew 16:24; emphasis added). The key to taking up our crosses, whether of our own making or be they crosses of the world is to "deny ourselves" and choose to follow Christ. It does no good to take up our crosses and not tread in His footsteps along the covenant path. The effectiveness of any vitamins we might have taken—chocolate-covered or not—is completely negated.

His Yoke

To restate our paradox: disciples are being invited to take on Jesus's yoke, which is described as light; and simultaneously being asked to take up their own crosses and the crosses of the world, which are certainly not light. Unquestionably, these concepts seemed unusual, even almost foreign, and presented theological challenges to the Jews living in Palestine, given that they were suffering under the heavy yoke associated with the scourge of Roman bondage (which included servitude, burdensome taxation, persecution, etc.). To have the Nazarene talk in terms of a yoke sounded like an additional, unwelcome burden, even though the Savior described His yoke as "easy" and "light."

For some twenty-first-century Latter-day Saints, these paradoxical statements may also be difficult to grasp because (1) unlike the former-day saints who were familiar with yokes as implements of everyday life utilized to carry food, water, and other commodities (see illustration below), we may not be able to comprehend and interpret the symbol's meaning since we probably haven't ever seen or used a yoke; and (2) we might not recognize the ways in which this commandment, which has never been rescinded, can be complied with in our modern world, resulting in the Lord's promised blessing: "Ye shall find rest unto your souls" (Matthew 11:29).

Furthermore, some might question relevance or applicability to the Saints today. We would do well to remember President Boyd K. Packer's counsel when speaking of the tree of life that Lehi saw in his grand vision: "You may think that Lehi's dream or vision has no special meaning [or relevancy] for you. But it does. You are in it; all of us are in it."[1] Likewise, "His yoke" and "our crosses" have significant meaning for each of us today as we move forward along the covenant path.

Perhaps a modern-day example will increase our understanding of yokes. Several years ago, I had a work assignment to visit a foundry in Western New York (USA), located not far from Palmyra, where the Prophet Joseph and his family lived during the formative and preparatory years preceding the Restoration. This foundry manufactures parts for railroad cars, the largest of which was a "yoke" (see illustration below). The yoke is molded out of iron and steel into a single unit and is then mounted around the wheels of the railroad car. Its primary function is to hold the wheels in such a position as to keep them aligned with the railroad track. The yoke's secondary function is to distribute the weight between the front axle and rear axle. The axle, which is symbolic of the cross bar of a yoke, cannot keep the wheels properly aligned on the track by itself. A yoke is needed.

Yoke in Ancient Times   Railroad Car Yoke

What is Christ's yoke? Three key elements of Christ's yoke come to the forefront: (1) having and adding to a knowledge of Jesus through studying His life; (2) keeping His commandments, a.k.a., "do[ing] the works of Abraham" (D&C 132:32); and (3) believing Christ, thereby increasing our faith in Him and His atoning sacrifice. Symbolically, Christ's yoke functions like the railroad car yoke in that as we learn of Him, we find ourselves aligned with God's will. In addition, we are enabled to stay on the "strait and narrow" covenant path leading toward the tree of life which bears the fruit of eternal life even though the mists of darkness and confusion arise in an effort to cause us to lose our way by leaving the safety of the path.

As a means of transporting things from one location to another, a yoke works most effectively if it is balanced across the shoulders of the person carrying the yoke. Too much weight on one side or the other makes it difficult to move forward toward a desired location. Distributing burdens evenly makes the task "easy." President Ezra Taft Benson observed that in the life of Jesus, "all the virtues were . . . *kept in perfect balance.*"[2]

Life's most difficult decisions are not necessarily between virtues that are good and vices that are evil but rather between two good things. The consequences of making choices between two goods are not trivial, especially when those choices are made without a sense of perspective and balance. We watch in awe as Olympic gymnasts compete on the balance beam with an incredible combination of grace and athleticism. Certainly, those highly skilled and masterfully trained athletes have learned the principles of balance. Self-confidence and humility, boldness and meekness, justice and mercy, assertiveness and kindness, the spirit versus the letter of the law, obedience and initiative, pruning and grafting, solemnity and good cheer, confidentiality and communication, remembering and forgetting, reproof and reconciliation—seeking and finding balance between these requires us to do as the Savior did: keep virtues in perfect balance. Being able to identify and follow the Savior's pattern to attain a perfect balance of salvific virtues (vitamins) is one of our tests in mortality. The gifts of His yoke and our crosses seem to be treasures beyond measure.

Another message resonating from the image of His yoke is the doctrine emphasized in the teachings of Alma at the waters of Mormon: "as ye are desirous to . . . *bear one another's burdens*, that they may be light" (Mosiah 18:8; emphasis added). Struggling with just our own burdens is an inappropriate and, in many cases, unsuccessful use of His yoke. On the other hand, when we put "our" burdens on one side of the yoke and place someone else's burdens on the other side, it becomes balanced and lighter to carry and more manageable to navigate our journey. The ultimate form of Christian service is to adhere to the counsel given to Frederick G. Williams, a counselor to Joseph Smith in the First Presidency, who was told in a revelation how to do the greatest good for all people around him:

And in doing these things *thou wilt do the greatest good unto thy fellow beings* and wilt promote the glory of Him who is your Lord.

Wherefore, be faithful; stand in the office which I have appointed unto you; succor the weak, lift up the hands which hang down, and strengthen feeble knees. (D&C 81:4–5; emphasis added)

It has been my experience that when taking upon ourselves His yoke and limiting the load carried by His yoke to just our own burdens, the task of rendering service to help our brothers and sisters is infinitely more difficult. Christ's yoke is light because if we place our trust in God, accept the covenants associated with His gospel plan, and center our faith in Jesus, we will be blessed with grace which will "make weak things become strong unto them" (Ether 12:27) and we will "do the greatest good unto our fellow beings" (D&C 81:4).

We Need Both Yokes and Crosses

Contrary to what some voices are saying today, Christ's yoke and our crosses are essential and vital ingredients in the process of becoming like Him. There are "philosophies of men mingled with scripture"[3] that would cause us to wander away from the covenant path described in Lehi's dream. Some are asserting that His yoke can and should be modified, changed, or improved on. Other voices proclaim that His yoke and our crosses are no longer necessary and can be eliminated. This latter false notion is reminiscent of Lucifer's response to the Father's query, "Whom shall I send?" wherein Lucifer announced, "Behold, here am I, send me, I will be thy son, and I will redeem all mankind, that one soul shall not be lost" (Moses 4:1). Satan's yoke would have resulted in loss of our agency. Hence, the Father announced that Christ would be sent as the implementer of the Plan, "for he [Lucifer] knew not the mind of God" (Moses 4:6). What did Satan not know about the mind of God? Yokes and crosses are a vital part of the plan of salvation, and Lucifer wanted no part of all the sufferings that would be entailed for him to come as God's son into a mortal world and endure the sufferings and pains associated with an infinite atoning sacrifice. Attempts to modify, improve on, or eliminate the taking up of Jesus's yoke and our crosses have been going on for centuries, to no avail.

The "strait and narrow covenant path" is perfectly designed to allow each of us who enter to move forward toward the tree of life carrying His yoke and our crosses. That path is neither too narrow or wide, nor full of curves that cannot be carefully and successfully navigated on our journey to the tree and partaking of its fruit. Modifying or changing His yoke would create transportation problems for us along the path. Remember the Savior entered onto the path by going through the gate of baptism; He clung to the iron rod, which is the word of God: "My doctrine is not mine, but His that sent me" (John 7:16); and then He pressed forward along the path to partake of the fruit. As the great exemplar, He showed us how to successfully traverse the strait and narrow covenant path.

Accepting the assertion that His yoke and our crosses are part of the plan and key elements of God's declaration as to the purpose of mortality here on earth—"And we will prove them herewith, to see if they will do all things whatsoever the Lord their God shall command them" (Abraham 3:25)—it seems imperative that we figure out how to take up both crosses: ours and those of the world. In reality, it is a simple process. We must have a sincere desire and express our willingness to do so through fervent and frequent prayer. Having cultivated that deep desire, when we ask, the Lord will lovingly place Christ's personalized, custom-designed yoke upon our shoulders that will guide us in learning of Him. Then, accepting His yoke and finding it to fit perfectly, we willingly and joyfully take up our crosses.

Furthermore, bearing up under His yokes and our crosses helps us develop a reservoir of empathy for burdens others are dealing with. The Apostle Paul taught that as a necessary consequent of making our baptismal covenants, we should "bear one another's burdens, and so fulfill the law of Christ" (Galatians 6:2). Mercifully, the Son of God offers us deliverance from the bondage of our burdens, whatever the source, through the redeeming power of His atoning sacrifice, His suffering in Gethsemane, and the blood shed on the cross of Calvary.

In sum, our perspective is sharpened and our understanding of yokes and crosses is greatly enhanced by Elder Neal A. Maxwell, who shared the following valuable insight:

> Happily, the commandment "Take my yoke upon on you, and learn of me; for I am meek and lowly in heart" (Matthew 11:29) carries an accompanying and compensating promise from Jesus—"and ye shall find rest unto your souls." This is a special form of rest. It surely includes the rest resulting from the shedding of needless burdens: fatiguing insincerity, exhausting hypocrisy, and the strength-sapping quest for recognition, praise, and power. Those of us who fall short, in one way or another, often do because we carry such unnecessary and heavy baggage [burdens]. Being thus overloaded, we sometimes stumble and then we feel sorry for ourselves.[4]

Early on in this final dispensation, President Brigham Young recognized the importance of yokes and distinguished between the yoke of Jesus and the yoke of Satan:

The person that wears the yoke of Jesus and bears his burden [is the one who] loves the cause of truth and righteousness more than all else. . . .

The person that wears the yoke of Jesus, that has communication with the heavens, finds his [or her] yoke easy and his burdens light; he is the master of it. . . . All that men [and women] can imagine and a million times more, God has in store for us. If we are faithful, all is ours. If we trample sin and iniquity under our feet, then we are the masters, which makes the yoke easy and the burden light.[5]

They who try to serve God and still cling to the spirit of the world, have got on two yokes—the yoke of Jesus and the yoke of the devil, and they will have plenty to do. They will have a warfare inside and outside, and the labor will be very galling, for they are in direct opposition one to the other. Cast off the yoke of the enemy, and put on the yoke of Christ, and you will say that his yoke is easy and his burden is light. This I know by experience.[6]

Thus, there really is no paradox between yokes and crosses. They are seatbelts necessary to assist us in crafting our eternal souls to become unfallen and dwell in indescribable happiness as we navigate the coming days.

Notes

1. Boyd K. Packer, "Lehi's Dream and You" (Brigham Young University devotional, January 16, 2007), speeches.byu.edu.
2. Ezra Taft Benson, *An Enemy Hath Done This* (Salt Lake City: Parliament Publishers, 1969), 52–53; emphasis added.
3. Hartman Rector, Jr. "You Shall Receive the Spirit," *Ensign*, November 1973.
4. Neal A. Maxwell, "Meek and Lowly" (Brigham Young University devotional, October 21, 1986), speeches.byu.edu.
5. Brigham Young, in *Journal of Discourses*, 8:206–7.
6. Brigham Young, in *Journal of Discourses*, 16:123.

Chapter 3

"I Will Turn Away Your Captivity"

(Jeremiah 29:14)

You know, it is a wonderful thing to be faithful,
but a much greater thing to be both faithful and competent.
(Elder Richard L. Evans)[1]

Shortly after Lehi and his family escaped from Jerusalem, King Nebuchadnezzar of Babylon conquered Jerusalem in AD 587 and placed King Zedekiah on the throne. He also took back to Babylon the "flowers of Israel"—young princes and princesses and builders—some of Judah's best and brightest. Once in Babylon, these young Jews mourned deeply that they had been dragged away from their homes and families and were being held captive in a strange, idolatrous land. The prophet Jeremiah tells us that they had a saying among themselves: "The fathers have eaten a sour grape, and the children's teeth are set on edge" (Jeremiah 31:29). If we were to translate this expression into today's vernacular, it might be rendered as follows: "Our fathers have eaten jalapeños, and the kids' mouths are burning!" Through this metaphor, they were saying: "Our fathers made bad choices and were disobedient, and we are the ones who have to suffer. They would not listen to the Lord, and we are now held captive because of their wicked choices. It's just not fair for us to be punished for what they did." Now, before we examine the Lord's response to them, we should first consider how this situation might be applicable today. I believe that each of us, to some degree, is being held captive because of someone else's bad decisions. In a sense, we all have experienced or are experiencing our own personal Babylonian captivity.

For example, while serving as a bishop, I became acquainted with a sweet sister whose father was an alcoholic who drank heavily most of the time she was growing up. "Oh," I responded, "so now, as the adult child of an alcoholic parent, I'll bet that you find yourself living by certain unwritten rules. These rules include (1) Don't Talk, (2) Don't Trust, and (3) Don't Feel. Furthermore, I wouldn't be surprised if you think that it's your job to make sure you keep all the family secrets." Looking at me with large bloodshot eyes full of tears, she asked, "How did you know?" I explained that social scientists and clinical psychologists have tracked the effects of alcoholism over four generations. The first generation drinks, the second generation keeps the secrets, the third generation is the people pleasers, and the fourth generation is frequently overindulged and a bit spoiled. Sadly, it's human psychology. Every generation has their own Babylonian captivity problem—and it was not their fault!

Another sister who was struggling with severe clinical depression recounted to me, her bishop, part of a conversation she had with a professional counselor to whom I had referred her to get help. When the counselor asked her who in her family also had depression, she looked surprised and then responded that her mother and grandmother both struggled with depression. "Congratulations!" the counselor replied. "You've won the genetic lottery. This type of depression is in your DNA and it has been passed down through your family." Tragically, for her, she was being held captive by the painful effects of clinical depression—and again it was not her fault. She would be the one having to deal with it, even though she did not ask for it, nor did she choose it.

(As a note, both sisters, with help, successfully worked through and conquered their captivity.)

There are many ways we might find ourselves held against our will in a personal, emotional, or physical Babylonian captivity. For instance, we might have a spouse or child who has deeply hurt us in some way (e.g., straying from the covenant path). We might have had a business where an employee or associate cheated us. Or perhaps, someone's poor choices might have resulted in us being hurt in a painful accident or losing someone we love. Our captivity might begin with a well-meaning

Church leader saying something unkind to one of our children. Or it could be a disability or weakness that keeps us from doing everything we want. It might even be the loss of a job or financial hardship due to someone's mistakes. The grudges and anger we feel might even come from government policy or world pandemics (such as COVID-19). For many, watching the evening news creates despair given some of the inexplicable and seemingly destructive decisions made by politicians and leaders with which we disagree.

Unfortunately, other people's choices affect our lives and our happiness, and yet we are the ones having to face the consequences. Now, we might respond by saying, "Well, life isn't fair. I need to just get over it!" Because at those moments when we are hurting, we want everything to be fair. And part of our brain believes life should be fair. Good things should happen to good people and bad things should happen to bad people. For instance, the gospel teaches that if I keep the commandments, I will be blessed. I might translate "being blessed" into "If I am good, I expect to be protected from other people's bad things! If I pay my tithing, I should not be having financial problems. If I keep the word of wisdom, I should not get cancer. And I especially should not have to suffer because someone else did something stupid. [Please note that stupid cannot be explained; and more importantly, it cannot be fixed!] That is not fair. They should pay for their mistakes and leave me out of it!" And yet we end up suffering anyway.

In ancient Jerusalem, righteous prophets like Daniel and Ezekiel were also carried off captive to the very same Babylon as were the unrighteous children of Israel. They, too, were torn from their homes and forced to live among strangers despite their righteousness. Their fathers had eaten sour grapes, and they as children were now paying for it! So wouldn't we like to know what words of comfort and assurance the Lord had for those exiles in Babylon? And at the same time, what words of comfort and peace does the Lord have for us in our own personal captivity? Through the prophet Jeremiah, the Lord sent a wonderful message of hope and peace to those carried away captive against their will or subjected to a Babylon captivity by virtue of the actions of others. In Jeremiah 29:4–7 we find the following:

Thus, saith the Lord of Hosts, the God of Israel, unto all that are carried away captives, whom I caused to be carried away from Jerusalem unto Babylon;

Build ye houses, and dwell in them; and plant gardens, and eat the fruit of them;

Take ye wives, and beget sons and daughters; and take wives for your sons, and give your daughters to husbands, that they may bear sons and daughters; that ye may be increased there, and not diminished.

And *seek the peace of the city* whither I have caused you to be carried away captives, and pray unto the Lord for it: *for in the peace thereof [the city] shall ye have peace.* (emphasis added)

In other words, the prophet Jeremiah is saying, "Keep living full lives. Seek happiness and peace by doing all the things people would normally do. Do not allow the bad decisions of other people to stop you from living a healthy, productive life." There is our great challenge! Amid our personal Babylonian captivity, the Lord is telling us to seek for and find peace because He has put it there. I don't know about you, but at times, that feels like a lot to ask! At those moments, peace, joy, and happiness might seem a million miles away. Just how are we supposed to seek for and find peace?

Grief

Finding peace in our Babylonian captivity first requires that we fully grieve our losses as a precursor to forgiveness. When we agreed to enter mortality, it was with the idea that the spectrum of our experience would be a mix; the ordinary would combine with the wonderful and the painful. Earth life, in its fallen state, is full of thorns and noxious weeds. For instance, when we open our hearts to love, we realize that others may hurt us at some point along the way. Imperfect mortal beings, intentionally or not, say and do things that cause pain. Yet to avoid such pain, we wall ourselves off from loving and being loved. The solution is to grieve momentarily and then choose to love by forgiving even though we might possibly be hurt anyway.

We would do well to remember that this mortal existence and proving ground is not eternal. True, it is Babylon—a lone and dreary world—but it is *temporary*. People grow old and die. Things end. A few verses later in Jeremiah 29, the Lord promises: "After seventy years be accomplished at Babylon I will visit you, and perform my good work toward you, in causing you to return to this place [Jerusalem]" (vs. 10). Yet pain, loss, and unfairness may abound while we wait patiently on the Lord. We expect one thing and get quite another. Whether it's someone we love, a situation, our health, or our hopes, we often lose what we really wanted to keep.

When we experience loss, we grieve. In fact, for us to remain healthy and emotionally deep people, we *must* grieve. There is a time to mourn; and mourn we must. One example of grieving exists among observant Jews, who have practiced it for centuries. When they mourn the death of a loved one, Jewish families and friends "sit shiva," which is seven days of official grieving. They take time to recognize their pain, grieve, and then move forward with their lives having properly initiated the healing process. Refusing to grieve—to withhold that natural reaction—causes our body to retain emotional pain.

Researchers have found that when we grieve or carry grudges, our bodies react with a stress response. That is, our brain determines there is a need to either fight or run from a perceived threat and thus prepares the body to defend itself. Under stress, the amygdala in the brain shuts down our immune system and injects cortisol and adrenalin into our blood system. This causes blood to flow into the large muscles of the body so that it can either fight or run. Consequently, blood moves from the creative part of our brain known as the pre-frontal cortex, to the back of our brain which directs the fight or flight response. One researcher remarked, "Stress makes people stupid."[2] This occurs because lack of blood to the creative section of our brain results in a mental fog, creating an inability to effectively solve problems or see things clearly. When we remain in this state for long periods of time, our physical health begins to be threatened. The increased levels of cortisol and adrenalin lead to an increased risk of heart disease, high blood pressure, and other undesirable maladies. Thus, when we are under stress, we are sicker and more at risk for long-term health problems. We are also less able to handle daily problems. In sum, when we fail to grieve, whether we recognize it or not, we place the body under unnecessary stress.

The same thing happens when we hold on to a grudge or remain angry at our emotional "Babylons." By remaining focused on the inequities of life or wrongs committed against us, we fail to grieve and let go. In this way, we provide a place for that unfairness to have a more permanent place in our brain. It is important to note that moving forward says nothing about the size of our past hurt or the impact it had on our life. It does not wait for justice to be served or a wrong to be avenged or an offending party to feel remorse or apologize. Grieving our loss is simply about finding peace in the city of our captivity, despite what has occurred in our life. It is about peace—our peace, which then brings us to gratitude, forgiveness, and healing.

There is another aspect of grieving which is important for me to point out. To grieve is to move closer to God—part of the process of being reconciled to Him—because we better understand His love and divine purposes. Satan tempts us to utilize his "separation strategy" to cope with our losses and pain. First, he beguiles us into mistakes, transgressions, and sins by tempting us to break laws and commandments. Second, in a truly ironic mode, he accuses us of having broken laws or commandments which he beguiled us into to doing! Third, he then accuses God for the problem, which he hopes that we will do also. Fourth, he accuses us for falling short of the gospel ideal. Finally, he introduces us to "shame," which can cause us to forget or at least be unclear about our true identity as children of a loving Father. Satan defines our worth in terms of our fallen past as promise breakers. We become awash in shame. What is Lucifer's remedy? Hide (recall Adam and Eve) or separate ourselves in other ways from God. He also introduces us to fear and then buffets us.

Christ's strategy, on the other hand, invites us to turn toward Him rather than hide. He then calls us to have faith, repent, and make covenants of salvation, which lifts us up and enables us to pass through the necessary grieving process. His eternal desire is to draw us to Him, which correlates with our desire for peace and forgiveness. He sends the peace the gospel gives, not as the world gives, through the ministering power of the Holy Ghost reassuring us that our goal is to return to the presence of God as an unfallen, perfect creature, a status we had in the premortal world. In contrast to Satan, Jesus defines us in terms of our future as joint heirs with Him in the celestial kingdom.

Gratitude

When we have been hurt, we form a story, a narrative, of what has happened to us. Such a narrative can either be a "grievance story" or a "gratitude story." In a grievance story, all we see is that we have gone through pain and its unfairness. We have been hurt deeply. In this story, we rationalize past injustices to explain why we are unable to do certain things now. We mistakenly limit our choices and believe that they shape our future. Also, we continue to mourn our past, believing things would be much different had the past never happened. Consequently, we remain a victim, still being held captive. We repeat this grievance story endlessly in our heads. Because it is a victim story, it impacts decisions we make on a regular basis. Thus, the Babylonian captivity in our head continues to define who we are and what we do. We repeat grievance stories to others, hoping they will empathize why we are what we are. That way, in sympathy, they will not be so judgmental about our failings! Consequently, the peace we are looking for usually remains out of our reach.

On the other hand, telling a gratitude story involves the very same events, the very same injustices. Only now, after we have fully grieved, we begin to see the course of our life through different eyes. In the gratitude story, we experience pain but we rise above it and live a peaceful life. We triumph regardless of our past. A gratitude story is a hero story, a "succeed despite the odds" story. It is an "I've been blessed with tender mercies" story. Life was hard, but now our world is much better. Finding peace and a lasting forgiveness happens when we wrap ourselves firmly in a cloak of gratitude. Gratitude becomes the healing balm that softens our hearts and opens our eyes to the good things that have happened to us. It puts us in a place where we receive gifts graciously, thank others easily, and share kindness consistently. Grateful people, it turns out, are healthier, have fuller relationships, and feel much less stress.

Grateful people tell gratitude stories. They repeat these stories to themselves and often share them with others. They openly express gratitude to others they meet. It becomes their narrative of life. True, they still live in Babylonian captivity. They are still surrounded by people with different values who perhaps continue to choose all the wrong actions. All things considered, the exiled children of Israel longingly wished that they were back home in Jerusalem. However, they became grateful for the beauties of the city and the kindnesses of people they met, they grew gardens, they had grandchildren, etc. In other words, they were able to recognize the good things they were blessed with. They enjoyed their homes and those around them.

The more we cultivate our attitude of gratitude, we find ourselves rising above Babylonian captivity. At that point we are no longer victims. Instead, we begin to see that we have thrived regardless of other's bad choices. And we have no doubt that our success is due, in large part, to wonderful people who comprise our circle of loved ones, both family and friends, and the Lord's tender mercies. Our lives then focus forward rather than backward. We find ourselves jettisoning Satan's "separation strategy" and emerging from the awful grip of shame. Gratitude allows us to be more resilient during mortality's trials and to be buoyed up with helpful friends as we do so.

Forgiveness

Finally, the result of gratitude is that we forgive. Developing the gift of forgiveness is as close to charity (the pure love of Christ, meaning His providing forgiveness to everyone who repents and comes unto Him) as we can achieve in this life. Certainly, a worthwhile endeavor, forgiving is an ongoing process here in mortality, not an event. C. S. Lewis shared this powerful insight:

> We call them fiends and feel that we need not forgive them. But, in reality, [when we develop] the power to forgive, we have lost the power to condemn.[3]

To which I would hastily add: *By continuing to condemn, we lose the power to forgive.*

One of my favorite stories about forgiveness involves an eighteenth-century singer and actress named Susannah Maria Cibber, who is remembered immortally for her many performances in the *Messiah*, which was presented to the public for the first time in Dublin, Ireland, in 1742. She is intricately tied to the first performance of Handel's masterpiece, which provided a wonderful setting for forgiveness, as it is the single most loved musical composition of all time that is closely associated with the Savior. Susannah acted and sang. Her voice was not particularly strong; however, she put such sincere feeling into everything she vocalized that audiences were entranced and moved by her singing. It was written and said of Susannah that her vocalizations penetrated the heart, not the ear, by connecting to the words or role she played. Handel discovered her, and though he was not generally patient with singers, he took extra pains to work with Susannah. Astonishingly, she could not read music.

She was born Susannah Arne, marrying Theophilus Cibber under intense pressure from her ambitious brother and father, who thought they would profit from the marriage. Theophilus was an actor and manager of a well-known theater in London on Drury Lane. He was a hard-drinking, womanizing, gambling man who already had sent his first wife to the grave. He promptly began to profit from his new wife, going so far as to take all of Susannah's jewelry and costumes in a drunken rage to help cover his gambling debts. Susannah was ravaged by the death of two infants, and Theophilus gave her a venereal disease. He began to pressure her into receiving the attentions and gifts of male callers who hung around the theater. Susannah refused, knowing what they ultimately wanted. When Theophilus brought the son of a wealthy squire named William Sloper to meet Susannah, the outcome was not what he fully anticipated. Happy to encourage their affair, provided he continued to get the money she earned from performing, Theophilus was enraged to learn that the gentle nature of William and Susannah's need for sincere love and caring produced first a sincere and deep affection and, eventually, love. Susannah asked for a divorce and ran away with William when it was refused.

A daughter was born, and Theophilus sued the Slopers for a fortune. It became the trial of the century, full of the sensationalism so loved by the British press and public. Theophilus won, but the court awarded him the tiniest sum for injury it could, knowing his nature. It was a victory in some ways for the Sloper family; but, in order to win, the lawyer had to decimate Susannah's character, completely destroying her reputation. A salacious book was written based on the infamous trial, which further ridiculed and shamed her, portraying Susannah as a seductress. Her career as a singer and actress on the London stage was over. William and Susannah moved to the English countryside to raise their daughter.

At roughly the same time, Handel's own success in London was waning. From a friend named Charles Jennens, he received the scripture compilation that would inspire him to write the music to the *Messiah*. Discouraged with the dwindling London audiences, Handel accepted an invitation to perform a season in Dublin, bringing the new oratorio with him. This same year, a close friend of Susannah, James Quinn, invited her to perform with him in Dublin, which included acting in several Shakespearean plays. Thus, the famous composer and the shamed singer plunged together to create music history. Handel gave Susannah the longest aria in the *Messiah*, written for her voice range and based on Isaiah's words:

He was despised and rejected of men; a man of sorrows and acquainted with grief. (Isaiah 53:3)

[He] gave [his] back to the smiters, and [his] cheeks to them that plucked off the hair: [he] hid not [his] face from shame and spitting. (Isaiah 50:6)

It is the moment in the oratorio which most demands intense emotion; and Susannah's voice and life experiences combined with powerful effect. The first performance in Dublin was scheduled for the Easter season. On the afternoon of April 13, 1742, Susannah sang the words and music that only she could comprehend and appreciate in a personal way. She sang as if her soul were connected to that of her Savior, aware in a profound manner of what Jesus had suffered and yet He forgave.

In the audience at the matinee performance was Dr. Patrick Delaney, the chancellor of St. Patrick's Cathedral in London, a highly respected clergyman. Having recently lost his wife, Dr. Delaney's emotions and feelings were particularly sensitive and tender. Moved deeply by Susannah's performance, he arose from his seat as she concluded her aria and called out to her on stage, his voice filling the music hall. "Woman, for this, be thy sins forgiven thee!" It was a turning point for Susannah. "Seest thou this woman?" Jesus had once asked Simon the Pharisee. Dr. Patrick

Delaney saw the woman—not her sins, not her shame, not the scandal. Forgiveness is a beautiful thing, a life-changing and enriching gift.

Susannah returned to the London stage, singing in the first performance of the *Messiah* there, as well as many of Handel's other compositions. In time, her career was resurrected as she continued to sing and act, becoming one of the greatest actresses to perform on the London stage. When he died, Handel was buried in Westminster Abbey in Poet's Corner, one of the most singular honors that can be bestowed by the British people. Susannah rests not far from him.[4]

The word "deliver" and its derivatives such as "deliverance" are found thirty times in the Old Testament, twenty times in the New Testament, fifteen times in the Book of Mormon, and fifteen times in the Doctrine and Covenants. There exists no doubt nor can it be a mystery to us that the Lord "will turn away [our] captivity" regardless of what caused or contributed to our being captive in personal Babylons (see Jeremiah 29:14). And while in that undesirable location, it is alright to grieve for a while, so that we are prepared to truly forgive. And through our sincere expressions and heartfelt actions of comfort and forgiveness, we obtain a tremendous blessing—we lose the power to condemn. Thankfully, our crosses and Christ's yoke become light. However, if we continue to condemn, we will lose the power to forgive and our crosses become even heavier burdens. Remember also that one person's (Dr. Delaney) expression of forgiveness led ultimately to a whole nation granting forgiveness.

Notes

1. Richard L. Evans, address given at the Northwest Inland Division Gathered for Zion's Camp, October 15, 1971.
2. Daniel Goleman, *Emotional Intelligence: Why It Can Matter More Than IQ* (London: Bloomsbury, 2009), 149.
3. C. S. Lewis, *God in the Dock: Essays on Theology and Ethics*, ed. Walter Hooper (Grand Rapids, MI: William B. Eerdmans, 2014), 5.
4. Adapted from S. Michael Wilcox, *Twice Blessed: The Beauty of Forgiving and Forgiveness* (Salt Lake City: Deseret Book, 2016).

Chapter 4

Less-Than-Divine Answers

Believe in order to understand,
rather than understand in order to believe.

(Saint Anselm)[1]

We should not discount or trifle with the answers we receive in prayer regardless of any doubts, uncertainty, or opposition that might rush into our soul after saying "amen." Elder Jeffrey R. Holland teaches us,

> If it was right when you prayed about it and trusted it . . . it is right now. Don't give up when the pressure mounts . . . certainly don't give in to that being [Satan] who is bent on the destruction of your happiness. He wants everyone to be miserable like unto himself. Face your doubts. Master your fears. *"Cast not away therefore your confidence."* [Hebrews 10:35] Stay the course and see the beauty of life unfold for you.[2]

Unfortunately, there are times when it was not right in the first place. Answers can be received from sources other than the Lord. Elder Hartman Rector related the following experience:

> Two young returned missionaries came to see me one time and said that they'd both prayed, and they'd both gotten the same answer—they were supposed to marry the same girl. I said, "I want to see the girl."

And so that beautiful [young woman] came to my office; it was very obvious to me how they got that answer. I asked her how she felt about the two elders.

She said, "I don't want anything to do with either one of them!"[3]

Sadly, in the Church, such matrimonial "mis-revelations" are legendary. There are many stories of those who claim to have received a "revelation" for someone else. In a much darker sense, there were also many situations from the earliest days of the Church of those who have claimed revelations about the Church, the Second Coming, plural marriage, etc. Dig to the bottom of most any apostate group, and we usually find an alleged "vision," "dream," or "revelation." The scriptures are replete with charismatic Korihors who declare the Church in the wrong while they, alone, have the answers.

There have been numerous cases of revelations being received that are not so divine. Over the course of time, these generally pale, but sinister imitations disrupt sincere efforts to get answers and make righteous decisions. They are Satan's efforts to sever or disrupt the lines of communication with God. Studying the early history of the restored Church, we sadly learn of spiritual mayhem experienced by the Saints in Kirtland. Many manifestations were bizarre, disruptive, and clearly inspired by the adversary. Joseph Smith inquired of the Lord on how to educate, without offending, these new converts. In response, he was told:

> *Ye are commanded in all things to ask of God*, who giveth liberally; and that which the Spirit testifies unto you even so I would that ye should do in all holiness of heart, walking uprightly before me, considering the end of your salvation, doing all things with prayer and thanksgiving, *that ye may not be seduced by [1] evil spirits, or [2] doctrines of devils, or [3] the commandments of men. . . .*
>
> Wherefore beware lest ye are deceived; and that ye may not be deceived seek ye earnestly the best gifts. (D&C 46:7–8; emphasis added)

False revelations can come from any one of three sources: evil spirits, doctrines of devils, and commandments of men. Hence, we are to ask

God and seek the best gifts of the Spirit to have appropriate and sufficient discernment. Let's briefly examine these three improper sources of seemingly correct answers, thus preventing false answers from entangling us in wrong information.

Evil Spirits

Elder Hugh B. Brown described vividly the Friday night before the Saturday session of general conference where he would be sustained as a member of the Quorum of Twelve Apostles. By virtue of owning some acreage where oil had recently been discovered, he was about to become quite wealthy. Rather than experiencing a sense of rejoicing, he began to feel depressed and shrouded in confusion, uncertainty, and darkness. Among other things, he worried about the effect sudden wealth might have on his family. Elder Brown recalled:

> I went in the bedroom alone and there, through the night, I had the most terrible battle with the powers of the adversary. . . . Sister Brown came in later in the night, toward morning in fact, wanting to know what was the matter. And when she closed the door, she said, "What's in this room?" And I said, "Nothing but the power of the devil is in this room." And we knelt together by the bedside and prayed for release. We spent the night together, the balance of it. And in the morning I went down to my office. It was Saturday now and there was no one at the office. And in going into the office, I knelt by a cot and asked God for deliverance from the darkness that had enveloped me. And coming from somewhere there was an element of peace, the kind of peace that rests on the souls of men when they make contact with God. And I called her and said, "Everything is all right, or is going to be!"[4]

There are times when the adversary attacks us directly with the help of his minions. These experiences are as real as they are terrifying. Anyone who has ever experienced contact with or communication from evil spirits has little doubt of the presence of darkness and foreboding. However, at times "satanic gifts of the spirit" can be more subtle and hard to distinguish from the real thing. This is one of the reasons President Nelson emphasized the importance of recognizing and obtaining personal revelation by studying the scriptures (especially the Book of Mormon) to learn how prophets, apostles, and Christ's disciples became proficient at receiving inspiration through the power of the Holy Ghost. When trying to influence mortals, evil spirits do not distinguish between those of good and bad moral character. They are "equal opportunity" devils. Gratefully, we are blessed to have the companionship of the Holy Ghost to guide us to the truth of all things and to recognize both the nature and the source of gifts.

Doctrines of Devils

What are the doctrines of devils? Paul helps us identify them:

> Now the Spirit speaketh expressly, that in the latter times some shall depart from the faith, giving heed to seducing spirits, and *doctrines of devils*;
>
> Speaking lies in hypocrisy; having their conscience seared with a hot iron;
>
> Forbidding to marry, and commanding to abstain from meats, which God hath created to be received with thanksgiving of them which believe and know the truth. (1 Timothy 4:1–3; emphasis added)

Doctrines of devils are those doctrines originated by the "father of lies." They are falsehoods and untruths that come wrapped in godly-looking paper, seemingly tied up with a bow of truth. One Latter-day Saint scholar writes that all kinds of lies and partial truths would be taught by false teachers who would "speak lies in hypocrisy" (1 Timothy 4:2). Continuing, he says:

> Knowing full well that their words are false, they will yet send them forth because they are pleasing to the carnal mind . . . doctrines such as " . . . forbidding to marry, and commanding to abstain from meats . . ." sound noble and God-given to some, even though living prophets declare otherwise. Lies that can be

told, using the name of God, are powerful deceivers, even to the very elect.[5]

President Harold B. Lee warned:

These misguided, uninspired, man-appointed leaders would blaspheme God's name and his tabernacle and would make war on the saints and even kill them; all the while thinking they were doing God a service. (John 16:2.) [The Savior] made it clear, however, that any such institution so established, if it were not built upon his gospel, would have success and joy in their works for a season but by and by the end would come and they would be hewn down and cast into the fire from whence there is no return.[6]

Satan and his minions will only be successful "for a season." However, a great deal of damage can and will be done in that season. There is great pain and loss for those who follow these lies only to discover their falsehood farther down the road. By this time, bad decisions have been made, lives altered, and Saints have strayed from the covenant path. Only when the light shines fully on these follies is the full extent of the deception realized.

How do we know when an apparent inspiration or prompting is, instead, a doctrine of the devil? One sure way to know is when it leads us to paths contrary to what the prophet and the Church currently teach. Personal revelations that direct us to "higher" or "special" callings, to things the rest of the Church is not "prepared for," are doctrines of the devil. They appeal to the vanity of its recipients and are seductive in their appeal. They also harden hearts and make it difficult for the deceived to hear the Giver of Truth.

I am aware of a devoted youth leader. He magnified his calling and helped make activities fun and meaningful. Friendly and outgoing, he was involved in many leadership positions. Then, tragedy struck. With little warning, his wife of ten years left him and their three daughters. When he finally located her, she had joined a fringe group that was still clinging to the practice of plural marriage. She explained to him that she had received a "revelation" that she was supposed to live a "higher law." The rest of the Church was just not prepared to do so presently. She explained that this would involve certain "sacrifices," such as abandoning her family, which she was now prepared to make. Elder Oaks warns against those:

> Other voices are the bleatings of lost souls who cannot hear the voice of the Shepherd and trot about trying to find their way without his guidance. Some of these voices call out guidance for others—the lost leading the lost.[7]

Commandments of Men

We are blessed with the gift and guidance of the Holy Ghost so we will not be deceived by the "commandments of men." Specifically, we can be deceived by the commandments of other men and women, and we can be deceived by ourselves, the natural man. Let's look first at the commandments of others; then we will examine the commandments of ourselves.

Commandments of Others

One of the leadership challenges Joseph Smith faced early in the Church was his age. He was younger and less educated than many of the male converts in the Church. "You consider me a boy with the rest of you," he told the men of Zion's Camp. "You have not realized my position before the Lord."[8] Joseph's youthfulness sometimes caused him to be swayed by older and seemingly more educated and sophisticated colleagues such as Sidney Rigdon and Martin Harris. This was never more evident than in the case of the loss of the 116 pages of the Book of Mormon manuscript. He had repeatedly gone to the Lord trying to secure permission for Martin Harris to take the manuscript home to show his wife. After it was lost, Joseph was severely reprimanded by the Lord:

> And behold, how oft you have transgressed the commandments and the laws of God, and have *gone on in the persuasions of men.*
>
> For, behold, you should not have feared man more than God. (D&C 3:6–7; emphasis added)

Joseph had allowed his prayers to be tempered by his desire to please the older Martin Harris.

We encounter a similar problem when others pressure us to get an answer that would please them. This can occur, for instance, when a young man informs a young woman that she is to be his wife. If her search for her own confirmation is heavily influenced by her desire to please this young man, she may "fear man more than God." She may get the answer the young man wants to get because he wanted her to get it. How unfair that anyone would put such a burden on another, but it does happen far too frequently. For the rest of their lives, such young couples leave themselves open to questions about the legitimacy of their answer. This is an extremely sandy piece of real estate on which to build a home!

We can also be swayed by charismatic speakers or hyped-up, sales-type presentations. Nefariously crafted appeals can stir our emotions and cause us to make decisions we would not have made otherwise. In the process of making choices, with the words of the sales pitch still ringing in our ears, we can feel excited or motivated and mistake those feelings for the Spirit. Both Eve and her son Cain were persuaded by a smooth-talking snake-oil salesman. Both could provide testimonials to Lucifer's School of Dissemination of Falsehood, dressed in shiny packaging but devoid of contents of any real value.

Commandments of Ourselves

False inspiration can also come from listening to what our natural man or woman thinks we want. These self-fulfilling revelations are always pleasing because they tell us exactly what we wanted to hear. Of all the sources of false inspiration, this may be the most difficult to discern. In attempting to distinguish between the Lord's answers and our own desires, we should consider these six questions, proposed by Elder Hartman Rector,[9] that can help us determine the source of our inspiration:

#1 Is it within the bounds and limitations of your calling, and does it require service consistent with your calling?

In other words, is the answer intended only for us or for those we have responsibility over? When we receive answers for someone else's stewardship we can be assured they are not from God. He does not work that way.

#2 Is it consistent with the revealed word of God?

As discussed above, doctrines of devils can look like inspiration, but they subtly lead to paths opposite from the revealed word of God. Answers that gratify our pride or exalt us in the eyes of others are the kind of answers Satan knows will appeal to our vanity and pride. Hidden or secret knowledge, unavailable to the rest of the Church, is not consistent with established patterns of the kingdom of God on earth.

#3 Is the receiver of the communication a fit receptacle?

This question is not only about repentance, it is also about the desires of our heart. Are they aligned with the will of our Father in Heaven? When we sought our answer, had we already decided that we were totally willing to submit to whatever the Lord would direct, or did we approach Him with a limited list of things we were willing to do? Or, perhaps, did we specify a time frame in which the answer must arrive and be acted on? Preconceived notions not sourced from the Holy Ghost render us as unfit receptacles.

#4 Does the communication edify and cause you to rejoice?

Whenever we are in contact with the Spirit, we always experience an increase of love. The love of Christ fills us and will aid us in what we have been directed to do. Answers that leave us depressed, sad, or angry should be seriously questioned. Sometimes the answer will direct us to do things that will have some mixed emotions to them, like needing to move away from family or a beloved ward. However, in receiving that answer, the Lord will immediately comfort us with an outpouring of love, knowing what lies ahead. Answers devoid of the Spirit will have no accompanying love, only negativity.

#5 Does it cause your bosom to burn or speak peace to your soul, or are you left troubled by the communication?

The Holy Ghost is the Comforter the Savior promised to those who have faith, repent, and are baptized by immersion by someone with His priesthood authority. The Comforter will provide peace to our hearts as true answers are received. Answers from other sources cannot duplicate heavenly peace; this feeling of love is unique to divine confirmation.

#6 Is the communication vivid to the understanding, or does it leave a cloud or a hazy impression?

Spiritual answers give us a calm, clear path to follow. They expand our mind as we understand what we are to do. This is generally accompanied by a sense of relief as our conflict is resolved. This is true even if the answer is contrary to what we expected—the calm is the same. When the legendary returned missionary declares to the young woman that he just met on campus that he has had a revelation stating she agreed in the premortal existence to be his wife, a number of conflicting things are occurring. To his credit, he is doing what he is supposed to be doing—finding a wife and starting a family. He is also attempting to rely on the Spirit in his decision making. These are both worthy goals. Unfortunately, though, he has also confused his own emotions and desires with the workings of the Spirit. By doing so, he has uttered divine declarations he had no right to make. He has not yet understood how the Spirit works.

Separating out our own emotional reactions from the calming presence and influence of the Holy Ghost requires experience and the gift of discernment, which is a gift of the Spirit for which it is our privilege to ask. There is a dramatic difference between the excitement we might feel when we have decided to do something and feelings that "speak peace to your soul" as Elder Rector describes. We should also be alert that both can occur. In fact, reactions of joy can follow the Spirit's confirmation provided we identify which came first. Danger lurks when we feel our excitement *first*, then offer a prayer telling the Lord what we are going to do. Not a good plan!

Protection against Less-Than-Divine Answers

Finally, we can find ourselves anxious and worried as we try to distinguish spiritual answers from our own desires, doctrines of devils, or even evil spirits. This can lead us to constantly second guess each sensation manifested internally as we seek for truth. Thankfully, there does exist a way to protect against these false witnesses. Nephi describes the bravery of his father, Lehi, who courageously walked among the wicked citizens of Jerusalem and declared the unpopular message to repent when he was told to preach about the vision that he was shown. They responded as do most societies that are ripe for destruction: "they were angry with him" to the point that they "sought his life." However, regardless of bitter persecution, Nephi declared, "I, Nephi, will show unto you that the tender mercies of the Lord are over all those whom he hath chosen." How powerful are the Lord's tender mercies? Nephi explains that, for those called by the Lord, they are made "mighty even unto the power of deliverance" (1 Nephi 1:20). We know the rest of the story: Lehi and his family were preserved from the wicked plots of the Jews and were able to safely leave Jerusalem before it was destroyed by the Babylonians in 587 BC.

When we are bogged down in our own Winter Quarters, we grow anxious to break camp and resume the efforts of moving on toward the ultimate realization of promised blessings. We struggle, we plan, and we sort through the competing voices for the right path to follow. In those moments, if we will stop and ponder, the way will be illuminated before us and we will be delivered by God's tender mercies. Elder Bednar spoke powerfully on tender mercies when he declared:

> We should not underestimate or overlook the power of the Lord's tender mercies. The simpleness, the sweetness, and the constancy of the tender mercies of the Lord will do much to fortify and protect us in the troubled times in which we do now and will yet live. When words cannot provide the solace we need or express the joy we feel, when it is simply futile to attempt to explain that which is unexplainable, when logic and reason cannot yield adequate understanding about the injustices and inequities of life, when mortal experience and evaluation are insufficient to produce a desired outcome, and when it seems that perhaps we are so totally alone, truly we are blessed by the tender mercies of the Lord and made mighty even unto the power of deliverance.[10]

In other words, the more we are cognizant of the constant tender mercies the Lord provides, the less likely we are to be confused by other voices. They will sound shrill and self-serving in comparison. An awareness of these mercies' results will fill our heart with gratitude and awe to the loving Father who provides them. In that moment filled with love, there can only be truth.

Notes

1. Saint Anselm, in *Saint Anselm: Basic Answers*, trans. Sidney Norton Deane, 2nd ed. (LaSalle, IL: Open Court Publishing, 1962), 7.
2. Jeffrey R. Holland, "Cast Not Away Thy Confidence" (Brigham Young University devotional, March 2, 1999), speeches.byu.edu; emphasis added.
3. Hartman Rector, Jr., "How to Know If Revelation Is from the Lord" (Brigham Young University devotional, January 6, 1976), speeches.byu.edu.
4. Hugh B. Brown, "Eternal Progression" (Church College of Hawaii address, October 16, 1964), 8–10.
5. Bruce A. Van Orden, *Studies in Scripture, vol. 6: Acts to Revelation*, ed. Robert Millet (Salt Lake City: Deseret Book, 1987), 187–88.
6. Harold B. Lee, *Decisions for Successful Living* (Salt Lake City: Deseret Book, 2009), 66.
7. Dallin H. Oaks, "Alternate Voices," *Ensign*, May 1989.
8. Wilford Woodruff, in Conference Report, April 1898, 29–30.
9. See Rector, "How to Know If Revelation Is from the Lord."
10. David A. Bednar, "The Tender Mercies of the Lord," *Ensign*, May 2005.

Chapter 5

Grace: God's Gift to Change Us from Fallen to Unfallen

I believe that the Sun has risen, not only because I see it,
but because by it I see everything else.

(C. S. Lewis)[1]

A priesthood leader (we will call him Bishop Kendall) shared with me part of a conversation which he had with one of the members of the ward for which he had stewardship (we will call him Edward).

Edward: "Bishop Kendall, I just don't get grace."

Bishop Kendall: "What is it that you don't understand, Edward?"

Edward: "I know I need to do my best, and then Jesus does the rest. But I can't even do my best. I know that I'm supposed to do my part and then Jesus makes up the difference by filling the gap that stands between my part and perfection. But who fills the gap between where I am now and my part?"

Bishop Kendall then took a piece of paper and drew two dots—one at the top of the page representing God and one at the bottom of the page representing Edward.

Bishop Kendall: "Edward, would you please draw a horizontal line somewhere between the two dots depicting how much is your part versus how much is Christ's part?"

Edward took the piece of paper and, after thinking for a few moments, drew a line approximately in the middle of the page, and said, "That seems about right: half me, half the Savior." Then, before Bishop Kendall could reply, Edward drew another line about two-thirds of the way between the bottom dot and the line he had just drawn in the middle of the page. Seeing some uncertainty in Bishop Kendall's eyes, Edward quickly said, "That line is where I am now in relation to the line representing my part."

Bishop Kendall: "Edward, the truth is, there are NO lines. Jesus Christ filled the whole space. He paid our debt in full. He did not pay everything except for a few dollars. He paid it all. There is no gap. Jesus does not *make up* the difference. Christ makes *all* the difference. Grace is not about filling gaps. It is about filling us."

Edward: "Right, like I don't have to do anything?"

Bishop Kendall: "Oh no, you and I have plenty to do, but it is *not* to fill the gap. All of us will be resurrected. All will return to our Heavenly Father's presence. What is left to be determined by our obedience is what kind of body we plan on being resurrected with, how comfortable we plan to be in God's presence, and how long we plan to stay there. The gospel of Jesus Christ requires that each of us demonstrate faith, even exceeding great faith [which, by the way, each of us exhibited during our premortal existence], repent, make and keep the covenants associated with baptism, to receive the Holy Ghost, and to endure to the end.

"By complying, we are not paying the demands of justice—not even the smallest part. We are showing our appreciation for and acceptance of the atoning grace extended to us by God through the atoning sacrifice of Jesus Christ by using that precious gift to live a life like His. Jesus provides us with the opportunity for ultimate perfection and He will help us reach that goal. Because of the infinite atonement and sacrifice to meet the demands of justice, He can now turn to us with His own set of requirements."

Edward: "So, what's the difference? Whether our efforts [a.k.a., all we can do] are required by justice or Jesus, they are still required."

Bishop Kendall: "That's true; but our efforts are required for a *different purpose*."

Allow me to share a personal illustration that hopefully will enhance our understanding of *grace* and help us to grasp what that different purpose is. When my oldest daughter, Emily, was in fourth grade, she became involved in the school's music program, which resulted in her strong desire to play the flute. So, being a relatively good dad, I paid for flute lessons. Because Dad paid the tuition in full, it is perfectly reasonable that I would expect Emily to practice. Truthfully, though, I really did not have to ask her. Did Emily's practicing pay the flute teacher? NO. Did Emily's practicing repay Dad for paying the flute instructor? NO. *Practicing achieved a different purpose.* Over the ensuing years, the combination of gaining knowledge about how to read music—eighth notes, quarter notes, half-notes, whole notes, the symbols for louder and softer, faster and slower, learning how to hold the flute, how to work the keys, how to adjust the mouthpiece; all that and more that a masterful teacher shared—coupled with hours and hours of practice produced *proficiency.* Emily changed and *became* a talented and gifted musician. She became so proficient that during the years when Brother Ryan Murphy, currently the assistant conductor of the Tabernacle Choir at Temple Square, lived in her ward in the Boston area, he would walk into sacrament meeting with a sheet of music that he had composed during the week that was a flute accompaniment for the song that the ward choir would be singing that day, and Emily would play it virtually sight unseen. Emily changed from a ten-year old struggling to make lovely musical sounds into a talented flutist who now produces heavenly strains. Elder Bruce C. Hafen, Emeritus General Authority Seventy, wrote:

> The great Mediator asks for our repentance NOT because we must "repay" him in exchange for His paying our debt to justice; but because repentance initiates the developmental process [of being changed by Christ's grace] that, with the Savior's help, [results in our] becoming celestial persons.[2]

Elder Dallin H. Oaks explained it in this manner: "The repenting sinner must suffer for his/her sins, but this suffering has a different purpose than punishment or payment. Its purpose is CHANGE."[3] Put in terms of Emily's gaining skills, knowledge, and understanding through music lessons and practicing the flute, the purpose was not punishment or payment. Its purpose was *change.* Grace emanates freely from God, and the power of Christ's atoning sacrifice makes eternal change possible. What is that eternal change? It is being reconciled to God.

Paraphrasing a noted scholar, while many Christians view His suffering and dying merely as being a huge favor, Latter-day Saints recognize that infinite sacrifice as the ultimate investment He made in us. A life impacted by grace eventually looks like Christ's life.[4] As a third witness, Mormon taught his son (and us) that grace is not just about being saved. It is also about activating and sustaining the process of change to become like the Savior (see Moroni 7:2). Finally, Professor Hugh Nibley succinctly stated, "Work we must; but the lunch [grace] is free."[5]

Christ's Power to Change Us

The word *atonement* literally means "a state of reconciliation, healing, and reunion with God in which a man or woman exemplifies the attributes of God." Such a desirable reconciliation and reunion involves more than a change in our desires; it means that our human fallen nature must be replaced with a divine unfallen nature (see Mosiah 3:19 and 2 Peter 3:4). Changing our nature is beyond our capacity. It happens because the grace that God grants enables the mighty change from a fallen state to an unfallen state. Such a revamping of the natural man or woman is made possible only by and through the atoning sacrifice of Jesus Christ. C. S. Lewis provides additional insight:

> The road back to God is a road of moral effort, of trying harder and harder [our searching for, finding, and hearing the Master healer]. But in another sense it is not trying that is ever going to bring us home. All this trying leads up to the vital moment at which you turn to God and say, "You must do this. I can't." . . . And what matters is the nature of the change in itself, not how we feel while it is happening. It is the change from being confident about our own efforts to the state in which we despair of doing anything for ourselves and leave it to God.[6]

Continuing:

> I know the words "leave it to God" can be misunderstood. The sense in which a Christian leaves it to God is that he [or she] puts all their trust in Christ; trusts that Christ will somehow share

with him the perfect human obedience which He carried out
from His birth to His crucifixion; that Christ will make the man
[or woman] more like Himself . . . everything which really needs
to be done in our souls can be done only by God.[7]

God and man are working together in process of the salvation of the
human soul. The real question is *not* whether we are saved by grace or
works. The real questions are these: In whom do I trust? On whom do I
rely? In his poem "Invictus," William Ernest Henley described each man
and woman as being the "master of his fate" and the "captain of his soul."

Invictus

Out of the night that covers me,
black as the pit from pole to pole,
I thank whatever gods may be
for my unconquerable soul.

In the fell clutch of circumstance,
I have not winced nor cried aloud.
Under the bludgeonings of chance
my head is bloody, but unbowed.

Beyond this place of wrath and tears
looms but the Horror of the shade,
And yet the menace of the years
finds, and shall find, me unafraid.

It matters not how strait the gate,
how charged with punishments the scroll,
I am the master of my fate:
I am the captain of my soul.[8]

Elder Orson F. Whitney of the Quorum of the Twelve wrote this
resounding response:

The Soul's Captain

Art thou in truth? Then what of Him
who bought thee with His blood?
Who plunged into devouring seas
and snatched thee from the flood?

Who bore for all our fallen race
what none but him could bear,
The God who died that man might live
and endless glory share?

Of what avail thy vaunted strength
apart from His vast might?
Pray that His light may pierce the gloom
that thou mayest see aright.
Men are as bubbles on the wave,
as leaves upon the tree,
Thou, captain of thy soul! Forsooth,
Who gave that place to thee?

Free will is thine—free agency,
to wield for right or wrong;
But thou must answer unto Him
to whom all souls belong.
Bend to the dust that "head unbowed,"
small part of life's great whole,
And see in Him and Him alone,
the captain of thy soul.[9]

Two defining traits emerge when comparing "Invictus" and "The Soul's Captain"—namely, (1) unjustified and arrogant pride, and (2) mocking rejection of the atoning sacrifice of Jesus Christ, most certainly reminiscent of Satan's rejection of the plan. Will it require great effort on our part to trust God and His plan? Yes! Does it require great effort to submit to God's will and sacrifice our will on the altar? Yes! Must we demonstrate unqualified faith in Jesus Christ, the Messiah, and His atoning sacrifice Yes!

President David O. McKay taught, "Human nature *can* be changed, here and now." Then he quoted the following: "You do change human nature, your own human nature, if you surrender it to Christ. . . . *Only Christ can change it.*"[10] Understanding, accepting, and incorporating grace into our lives is the key. Let me further emphasize:

- If the gospel did not require faith and repentance, there would be no *desire* to submit our will to God allow Him to change it to correspond with His will.

- If the gospel did not require making baptismal covenants and receiving the Holy Ghost, then there would be *no way* to change. We would be left with only *our* willpower, having no access to *His* power. Nephi's brother Jacob taught, "It is by *his* grace . . . that we have power" (Jacob 4:7; emphasis added).
- If the gospel did not require endurance to the end, then there would be no *internalization* of change over time. It would be surface and cosmetic rather than sinking deep into our soul and forever becoming part of the fabric of the person Our Heavenly Father desires us to become. The apostle John wrote, "It doth not yet appear what we shall be: but we know that, when he shall appear, we shall be like him" (1 John 3:2).

Unfortunately, too many are becoming disenchanted, giving up on the Church and the gospel because they are distressed by or are constantly feeling inadequate for thinking that they are falling short, believing they can never fill the "gap." Sadly, they do not understand *grace*. Some point to the writings of Nephi, who said:

For we labor diligently . . . to believe in Christ, and to be reconciled to God; for we know that it is by grace that we are saved, *after all we can do.* (2 Nephi 25:23; emphasis added)

An initial reading of this verse might cause us to believe that grace is offered chronologically *after* we have completed doing "all we can do"— sometimes known as the celestial kingdom "checklist"—but this notion is demonstrably false. We receive innumerable manifestations of God's grace long before we come to that point, which we now know does not exist (a.k.a., the line between my part and Christ's part). The grace of God was intimately involved in our spiritual progress in the premortal world; and grace will be involved in our eternal progression in the postmortal world to come. It belittles God's grace to think of it only as a "cherry on top" added at the last moment as a mere finishing touch to what we have already accomplished on our own without any help from God. Grace is God's total participation in the process of our salvation and ultimate exaltation.

When we begin to comprehend grace, we realize that the blessings of Christ's atoning sacrifice are continuous, and His strength is perfect and sufficient for overcoming our weakness (see 2 Corinthians 12:9) and turning it into strength (see Ether 12:27). Christ is not waiting at the finish line once we have done "all we can do." He is with us every step of the way. Another insight from Elder Hafen is particularly reassuring:

> The Savior's gift of grace to us is not necessarily limited in time to "after" all we can do. We may receive his grace before, during, and after the time when we expend our own efforts.[11]

Grace is not a booster engine that kicks in when our fuel supply is exhausted. Rather, it is our constant source of energy. Grace is not the light at the end of the tunnel but the illumination which leads us through the tunnel. Grace is not only extended to us there and then, somewhere "down the road." It is available right here and now. Elder Boyd K. Packer has counseled us, "While the Atonement of Christ applies to humanity in general, the influence of it is individual, very personal, and very useful. . . . The Atonement is of immediate and very practical value in everyday life."[12]

Christ's Atonement Is Infinite

Christ's Atonement works in both directions. Before His Atonement could make us one with God again through grace, Christ had to be at one with us, sharing all the vicissitudes of mortality—sorrow, pains, grief, suffering, disappointments, and heartaches. Yet with all the temptations, trials, and adversity of the world pressing down upon Him while in the Garden of Gethsemane, Christ "resisted unto blood" (Hebrews 12:4) that He might not let sin into His being. In the words of Elder Neal A. Maxwell, "Jesus partook of history's bitterest cup without becoming bitter."[13]

Christ paid the complete price for sin. He paid more than any person would *ever need* to be redeemed and delivered from this fallen, mortal state to the unfallen, immortal state. Justice was completely satisfied for every one of Father's children. Comprehending the Atonement from the perspective of His sufferings "breaks our hearts," so that we become humble, teachable, and willing to be changed through repentance. Sometimes, however, instead of coming unto Christ with a broken heart and a contrite spirit, we shrink from His healing arms of love, which are always outstretched to provide us comfort and protection from the law of justice. We clench our fists with a determination that we will never again cause Him additional pain and suffering. Instead of becoming one with Christ, we attempt to make it right on own. We somehow try to pay the price of sin for ourselves rather than to cause Him to suffer. We ache to pay for that which we have done that we might be clean.

Eternal law does not allow the offering of something imperfect to pay for imperfections that would somehow make things perfect. We are unable to pay the price necessary to be made pure and clean. It is true that we may suffer *because* of our transgressions, and we may even suffer *for* our sins, but we cannot, in the end, *remove* our sins. The Atonement involves more than removing an infinite mass of sin; it entails an infinite stream of individuals with their specific needs. The prophet Zenos taught:

> Thou art angry, O Lord, with this people, because they will not understand thy mercies [grace] which thou hast bestowed upon them because of thy Son. (Alma 33:16)

St. Augustine wrote of his understanding of the relationship between grace and enduring:

> Grace includes not only the call to salvation, the impulse of faith to respond, the inspiring of a good will, but also . . . the gift of enduring to the end. Such being the decree of the unchanging divine will, backed by divine power, it is irresistible; the assurance of persevering in grace is therefore absolute and infallible.[14]

In sum, grace works!

Perils and Pearls of Grace Found in Christ's Atonement

Being in a fallen world, and knowing that Lucifer has designed many devices which resemble the holy things of God (placebos instead of real vitamins), we would do well to recognize and then avoid several of what I shall refer to as "perils of grace" as opposed to the "pearls of grace" (discussed below). Sadly, some tend to assume a variety of misunderstandings of God's great plan. Professor Adam Miller illuminates these perils:

Grace is not God's back up plan. Jesus is not Plan B. God's boundless grace comes first and sin is what follows. Grace is not God's response to sin. Sin is our embarrassed, improvised, rejection of God's original grace. . . . We have to stop looking at God's grace from the perspective of our sins; and, instead let sin appear in the light of grace. . . . Sin likes to think that it came first and that grace is God's stopgap response. This is exactly backwards.[15]

Let me briefly highlight three common misconceptions that seem to be prevalent among the Saints. First, Christ and the "Grace Gap." As we have learned from the discussion above, this notion involves a kind of works—righteousness model. We do all we can and expend all our efforts (a.k.a., works) to be saved, and *then* Jesus fills in the remaining deficit. In other words, we start at 0 percent, go as far as we can (for instance 80 percent), then Christ fills in the Gap to reach 100 percent. The correct model operates in the following fashion: We believe Jesus is the Son of God who came earth to redeem all humankind. That belief grows within us causing us to plant the seed of faith (see Alma 32) and repent of our mistakes, transgressions, and sins. Finally, we consummate a covenant with our Father in Heaven through the ordinance of baptism which actuates the promises and power of grace.

Second, "Timing of Grace" or the "After All We Can Do" notion. In this misguided concept, Jesus waits until and will only step in with His grace once we have expended every effort to live the gospel. This misguided notion is one of Satan's most nefarious falsehoods. Grace was activated when Jesus of His own free will made the covenant with His Father to accept the priesthood assignment to be the Savior and Redeemer of all God's Children. We know this because during the ensuing war with Lucifer and those who chose to follow him, Christ prevailed through the power of grace. Those of us who chose to endorse God's plan by covenant were recipients of that grace. Grace was and continues to be a part of the gospel preparation in the premortal world of spirits still awaiting their turn on earth. Grace is present here in mortality; and it will continue to be functional in the spirit world where those who have died await resurrection. Grace will be in integral part of the purposes and objectives of the millennial activities.

Third, "Earning or Qualifying for Grace." This situation involves preoccupation with performing sufficient "good" works on our own, which leads to forgetting that such acts are hollow unless accompanied by complete dependence on Christ. We cannot earn exaltation. We do not have the necessary grit, determination, and willpower to do the "works of Abraham" (D&C 132:32) and win the battle against Satan on our own. Furthermore, we are not opening and then making deposits into a "celestial savings account" from which we intend to make a huge withdrawal when standing at the judgment bar.

Another group of fake vitamins consists of several inappropriate perceptions of Christ's Atonement. For instance, one mother spoke of how disappointed her daughter was that she had received a rejection notice from Stanford Business School: "But she will be alright through the Atonement." One man prayed for months to be healed of a serious illness. Finally, having been restored to health again, he remarked, "It was the enabling power of the Atonement that did it." Another sister misplaced some jewelry that had once belonged to her grandmother. She later found the jewelry and commented, "For many days I pleaded in prayer to be able to locate my treasure, and finally the powers of the Atonement were applied in my behalf. I found them."

If we misconstrue the Atonement of Christ to be so broad, so expansive that it covers everything related to our mortal journey regardless of how major or minor the circumstance—if we treat His Atonement as the source of *all* blessings we receive from God—then it will gradually lose its meaning and full potential impact on our lives. The Atonement must be linked to the atoning blood (shed not only in Gethsemane but also on the cross) of the Savior, Jesus Christ, in our hearts, our conversations, and our teaching. President Russell M. Nelson has cautioned:

> It is doctrinally incomplete [and inaccurate] to speak of the Lord's atoning sacrifice by shortcut phrases, such as, "the Atonement" or "the enabling power of the Atonement" or "applying the Atonement" or "being strengthened by the Atonement." These expressions present a real risk of misdirecting faith by treating the *event as if it had living existence and capabilities independent of our Heavenly Father and His Son, Jesus Christ. . . .* There is no

amorphous entity called "the Atonement" upon which we may call for succor, healing, forgiveness, or power. Jesus Christ is the source. . . . The Savior's atoning sacrifice—the central act of all human history—is best understood and appreciated when we expressly and clearly connect it to Him.[16]

President Henry B. Eyring echoed and provided a second witness to the expression of President Nelson with his comment made during the "Face to Face with President Eyring and Elder Holland" broadcast, March 7, 2017:

> The Atonement was something Jesus Christ did. It's not a *thing* itself. He *atoned* for our sins and he paid the price to allow us to be forgiven and resurrected. So its what he did that qualified him to give us forgiveness, to change our hearts. And it's the Holy Ghost doing that, it's not the Atonement as if it's a *thing* itself. . . . The Atonement is something the Savior did.[17]

We recall the metaphor used by Jesus when describing the kingdom of heaven to the multitude: "Again, the kingdom of heaven is like unto a merchant man, seeking goodly pearls: who when he had *found one pearl of great price*, went and sold all that he had, and bought it" (Matthew 13:45–46; emphasis added). Seeking pearls of grace, we find several expressions in holy writ:

- Grace as favor or acceptance in God's eyes (see Genesis 6:8; 19:19; Exodus 33:13; 34:9; Luke 2:40)
- Grace as a blessing from God (see Psalm 84:11; 2 Corinthians 9:8; 13:14; Mosiah 18:26; 27:5; D&C 88:78)
- Grace as an outpouring of the Holy Spirit or other spiritual gifts (see Acts 4:33; Romans 12:6; Ephesians 4:7; Mosiah 18:16; D&C 46:15)
- Grace as blessings associated with one's lineage (see Isaiah 45:25; Amos 5:15; Zechariah 12:10; D&C 84:99)
- Grace as that which God gives to the weak, including strength to overcome and to endure (see Proverbs 3:34; 2 Corinthians 8:9; 12:7–10; James 4:5-6, 1 Peter 5:5; Jacob 4:7; Ether 12:27)

- Grace as that which brings salvation (see Ephesians 2:8; 2 Timothy 1:9; Titus 2:11; 1 Peter 1:13; 2 Nephi 10:24-25; 25:23; D&C 138:14)

Let us then, as Lehi pleaded, rely solely on "the merits, and mercy, and *grace* of the Holy Messiah" (2 Nephi 2:8; emphasis added). That was, is, and always will be the plan. In our dispensation, the Lord directed Joseph and the developing Church seventeen times with words to that effect. I cite just two: "It must be done according to the pattern [plan] which I have given unto you" (D&C 94:2) and "I will give unto you a pattern [plan] in all things" (D&C 52:14). Grace has always been a part of the plan and was divinely designed to enable us to fulfill the plan.

Elder Bednar teaches:

> The enabling and strengthening aspect of the Atonement helps us to see and to do and to become good in ways that we could never recognize or accomplish with our limited mortal capacity. I testify and witness that the enabling power of the Savior's Atonement is real.[18]

Years ago, radio stations developed a popular programming format. It consisted of a disc jockey (DJ) taking "requests" to play a favorite song from callers who were listening to the radio. However, there was one DJ who decided to distinguish himself from all other DJs by only taking "suggestions." Requests implied that the DJ would honor the request—this is not necessarily the case with suggestions. So, in the spirit of "suggestions," I would like to provide a list of suggestions (as opposed to requests) that might be useful in availing ourselves of God's grace.

RESOLVING to come unto Christ

A Roman Catholic philosopher wrote:

> According to the theological liberal, the Sermon on the Mount is the essence of Christianity, and Christ is the best of human teachers and examples. . . . Christianity is essentially ethics. But wait, what is missing here? Simply the essence of Christianity, which is *not* the Sermon on the Mount. When Christianity

was proclaimed throughout the known world [at the time], the proclamation (kerygma) was not "Love your enemies!" Rather, "Christ is risen!" This was not a new *ideal,* but a new *event,* that God became man, died, and rose for our salvation. Christianity is, first of all, not an ideal but something real, an event, news, the gospel, the "good news!" The essence of Christianity is not Christianity; the *essence of Christianity is Christ.*[19]

We come unto Christ not only to be taught but to be transformed. He is not only our Example but our Change Agent and our Benefactor. Jesus is not only a convenient resource but the indispensable and vital element in our quest for happiness here and eternal reward hereafter. There is no hope and no possibility of reconciliation with the Father except by and through the Savior.

Being RECONCILED to God through Christ

The Atonement is the supreme divine act of mercy and grace and condescension by which our Father and God opens the door to reunion with Him. In and through Adam, we partake of mortality and death. In and through Christ, our Mediator and Intercessor, we partake of immortality and, potentially, eternal (meaning God's) life. By means of Christ's Atonement, we are reconciled to the Father. By means of His Atonement, the finite is reconciled to the Infinite, the incomplete to the Complete, the unfinished to the Finished, the imperfect to the Perfect. The Atonement of Christ, as the ultimate act of grace, demonstrates the love of the Father for all His children. Jacob, brother of Nephi, gave us this unforgettable illumination: "Wherefore . . . be reconciled unto him through the atonement of Christ, his Only Begotten Son, and ye may obtain a resurrection, according to the power of the resurrection which is in Christ, and *be presented as the first-fruits of Christ unto God,* having faith, and obtained a good hope of glory in him" (Jacob 4:11; emphasis added).

Being RENEWED in Christ

The Book of Mormon contains powerful invitations to come unto Christ and be changed. Indeed, one who chooses Christ chooses to be changed.

This renewal is a conversion from worldliness to saintliness, from being lured by the lurid to being enticed by holiness. It comes to us by virtue of the cleansing blood of Jesus and through the medium of the Holy Ghost, who is the Sanctifier. After hearing their king's soul-stirring address, the people of Benjamin "cried with one voice, saying: Yea, we believe all the words which thou hast spoken unto us; and also, we know of their surety and truth, *because of the Spirit of the Lord Omnipotent, which has wrought a mighty change in us, or in our hearts*, that we have no more disposition to do evil, but to do good continually" (Mosiah 5:2; emphasis added). Like you, I have marveled at this example of a group of people being renewed in Christ. We cannot suppose, however, that these Nephites never sinned again; that would be impossible in this fallen sphere. No, they made mistakes and transgressed after having experienced the mighty change, *but they did not want to*. And thanks be to God, they and we will be judged not only by our works but also by the desires of our hearts (see Alma 41:3 and D&C 137:9).

Being REINSTATED in the family of God

The Fall distances us from righteousness and alienates from the family of God. The atoning sacrifice provides us the means for reinstatement into the royal family. Christ is the Father of our awakening into newness of life. As members of His family, we are expected to know who we are and act accordingly—to keep His commandments with fidelity and devotion and to take seriously our divine birthright as Christians. As the seed of Christ, we hearken unto the words of the prophets, look to Jesus for redemption, and publish peace after the manner of the Prince of Peace.

RELYING totally upon the merits and mercy of Christ

It goes without saying, that we are expected to receive the ordinances of salvation (e.g., baptism); work faithfully in the kingdom of God on the earth; perform acts of Christian service (a.k.a., ministering); and endure faithfully to the end. In sum, we are expected to do the works of righteousness. These things are necessary—they evidence our covenant with Christ to follow Him and keep His commandments. *They are necessary, but they are not sufficient*. We are not saved by works alone, no matter how many or good. We are saved because God sent His Son to shed His blood in Gethsemane and on Calvary "that all through him might ransomed be" (*Hymns*, no. 176). We are saved by the blood of Jesus Christ. Salvation does not come by the Church alone; and were it not for the Atonement given through the grace of God as a free gift, all men and women would unavoidably perish.

RETAINING a remission of sins

Book of Mormon prophets speak of remaining in a justified condition, of maintaining or retaining our spotless standing before God, even though we make mistakes and transgress. We may err after our baptismal covenant with God, but we have no desire to do so. That is, our heart, our affections, our desires have all been surrendered unto Christ, and we have no desire to stray from our binding salvific covenants with Him. We are taught to do two things (here I will paraphrase from King Benjamin's address in Mosiah 4): First, we should always remember and retain in our remembrance the greatness of God, His goodness and longsuffering toward us, humbling ourselves even to the depths of humility, calling upon the name of Christ daily, and *standing steadfastly in the faith of that which is to come*. Second, we are to impart of our substance to the poor, according to the temporal blessings with which we have been blessed. The result of engaging in these two elements reflects being filled with the love of God to serve others.

REJOICING in Christ

I rejoice that, in full accordance with the great plan of happiness, Adam fell that we might be (see 2 Nephi 2:25 and Moses 6:48), and because of that fall, we enter mortality to undertake the second phase of our eternal journey along the covenant path. I further rejoice in the Fall, for it resulted in the birth, death, and resurrection of Jesus Christ, which is the only means whereby our hearts might be cleansed, our souls might be transformed thereby becoming unfallen creatures to dwell with Christ and our Eternal Parents forever. I rejoice in being able to trust fully in the powers of the atoning sacrifice of Jesus Christ to reclaim, renovate, renew, regenerate, and reinstate each of us from our fallen condition to unfallen perfection in the realms of eternal glory.

"Walk with Me"

Matthew records the incident of Jesus walking on the water:

> Jesus spake unto them, saying, Be of good cheer; it is I; be not afraid.
>
> And Peter answered him and said, Lord, if it be thou, bid me *come* unto thee on the water.
>
> And he [Jesus] said *Come*. And when Peter was come down out of the ship, he walked on the water, to go to Jesus. (Matthew 14:27–29; emphasis added)

In Danish, the word for "come" is *kom*, which sounds and generally means the same as the English. However, there is an additional meaning that is not found in English. Instead of our English translation of *come* being interpreted to mean "walk toward me," in Danish *kom* means, "walk with me." Thus, we get a completely different perspective. Jesus beckoned Peter to *kom*, meaning not just to walk toward him but to *walk with Him*. Not only did Jesus walk on the water and eventually silence the storm, but he also enabled Peter to do the same. The miracle is not so much that Peter walked an undefined distance on the surface of the swirling, storm-driven waters of the Sea of Galilee. Most artistic renderings of this incident depict that Peter is only three or four steps away from the fishing boat before he begins to sink in the waves. I think he walked a considerable distance away from the fishing vessel and toward Jesus before fear of drowning seized him and he began to sink into the swirling water. As he cried out, "Lord, save me," he caught hold of Christ's hand. The miracle was that Peter walked *back to the boat, on the water, with the Savior*.

Recently, as I sat in the celestial room of the temple having just completed an endowment session as a proxy, the thought occurred to me: If Jesus Christ is at the center of the gospel and the temple, why doesn't the endowment rehearse the life of Christ? Why does the presentation devote considerable time detailing certain events involving Adam and Eve? As I pondered these questions, it dawned on me that the narrative of Jesus's life is the story of *giving* Heavenly Father's children the gift of His atoning sacrifice. The temple narrative of Adam and Eve is the story of God's family *receiving* Jesus's atoning sacrifice.

Because of Christ's atoning and infinite sacrifice, embodied in the suffering in both the garden and on the cross, we can learn from our mortal experiences without being condemned by them. Hence, the Atonement is not a doctrine of erasing black marks—it is the core doctrine which provides for our eternal development by strengthening and healing our weakness. "I give unto men weakness" (Ether 12:27). Please note that the word is "weakness" (singular), not "weaknesses" (plural), which is how many Saints have inadvertently and mistakenly read this verse. Our "weakness" is that we cannot save ourselves. Ultimately, God-given grace arising from the Son's atoning sacrifice makes the process of becoming like Jesus possible by protecting us (based on our choices using our God-given agency—there is no forcing us) while we learn from practice what the pure love of Christ really is. Grace is activated because we make sacred covenants in the temple. C. S. Lewis summarized it this way: "Everything which really needs to be done in our souls can be done only by God."[20] I have come to sense the need to balance a type of "divine discontent"—a healthy longing to improve—with what Nephi called a "perfect brightness of hope" (2 Nephi 31:20); the Spirit-given assurance that things will work out through Jesus Christ.

Even though I have stressed the notion that grace fills the gap and that there is nothing which we can do to save ourselves, may I suggest some vitamins to chew on sustain the process of being reconciled to God.

First, let the past go. If we have done all that we can to rectify misdeed or poor judgments of former times, then move on. The apostle Paul taught: "This one thing I do, *forgetting those things which are behind, and reaching forth unto to those things which are before*" (Philippians 3:13; emphasis added).

Second, simplify our lives and focus on essentials. We will not enjoy the quiet and soft whisperings of the Spirit if we continue to be immersed in the noise and chaos of the world. We cannot be an instrument of the Savior's peace if we are so busy and involved that we have neither the time, inclination, nor energy to "wist ye not that I must be about my Father's business?" (Luke 2:49).

Third, learn to be more patient. God is in the process of working on us. He is not finished yet. We must remember that there is a heavenly, not earthly, timetable involved in becoming perfect. Joseph Smith taught: "It is not all to be comprehended in this world."[21] Patience implies "waiting on the Lord" (Psalm 37:34) and is very closely related to having *hope* in the Lord (discussed elsewhere herein). Suffice it to repeat the words of Paul to the Galatians: "For we through the Spirit wait for the hope of righteousness by faith" (Galatians 5:5). To be impatient with God is to lose sight of the truth.

Notes

1. C. S. Lewis, *The Weight of Glory* (New York: Touchstone, 1996), 106.
2. Bruce C. Hafen, *The Broken Heart* (Salt Lake City: Deseret Book, 1989), 149.
3. Dallin H. Oaks, *The Lord's Way* (Salt Lake City: Deseret Book, 1991), 223.
4. Brad Wilcox, personal notes from Education Week talk.
5. Hugh Nibley, *Approaching Zion*, vol. 9, *The Collected Works of Hugh Nibley* (Salt Lake City: Deseret Book, 1989), 251.
6. C. S. Lewis, *Mere Christianity* (New York: HarperOne, 2001), 146.
7. Lewis, *Mere Christianity*, 193.
8. William Ernest Henley, "Invictus," in *Book of Verses* (1888).
9. Orson F. Whitney, "The Soul's Captain," *Improvement Era*, May 1926.
10. David O. McKay and Beverly Nichols, in David O. McKay, *Stepping Stones to an Abundant Life* (Salt Lake City: Deseret Book, 1971), 23.
11. Hafen, 155–56.
12. Boyd K. Packer, "Washed Clean," *Ensign*, May 1997.
13. Neal A. Maxwell, "Enduring Well," *Ensign*, May 1997.
14. Walter A. Elwell, ed., *The Evangelical Dictionary of Theology* (Grand Rapids, MI: Baker Book House, 1984, 2001), 909.
15. Adam S. Miller, *Grace Is Not God's Backup Plan: An Urgent Paraphrase of Paul's Letter to the Romans* (n.p., 2015), 3–4.
16. Russell M. Nelson, "Drawing the Power of Jesus Christ into Our Lives," *Ensign*, May 2017; emphasis added.
17. Henry B. Eyring, "Face to Face with President Eyring and Elder Holland," (broadcast) March 7, 2017.
18. David A. Bednar, "In the Strength of the Lord," *Ensign*, November 2004.
19. Peter Kreeft, *Back to Virtue* (San Francisco: Ignatius Press, 1986), 83.
20. Lewis, *Mere Christianity*, 193.
21. Joseph Smith, *Teachings of the Prophet Joseph Smith*, 348.

Chapter 6

Rescuing

O my Father, I entreat thee, let me see thy beck'ning
hand; And when straying, may I meet thee ere
I join the silent band. Guide me, Father, guide
me, Father, safely to the promised land

("I'm a Pilgrim, I'm a Stranger," Hymns, no. 121)

Early in the beginnings of "The Way,"* outsiders observed Christians incorporating faith and understanding from the parables taught by Christ into their daily lives. One such witness was Galen, the most famous medical doctor of the second century. He was also one of the first pagans to express positive things about Christians. Around AD 140, he wrote:

> Most people are unable to follow a demonstrative argument con-
> secutively; hence they need parables to benefit from them . . . just
> as now we see the people called Christians drawing faith from
> parables [and miracles] and . . . acting in a new way . . . and in
> their keen pursuit of justice, having attained a pitch not inferior
> to that of genuine philosophers.[1]

It is illuminating to note that in the second century Galen observed Christians building their faith (theology) on parables. Jesus was a

---

* "The Way" is the name applied initially by non-members—pagans and gentiles—and subsequently utilized by new converts and proselytes for the Church established by Jesus, and which ultimately spread throughout the Mediterranean basin by the valiant and, at that time, unprecedented missionary efforts of Paul, the twelve Apostles and other disciples during the first and second centuries AD.

metaphorical (a.k.a., parabolic) teacher. That is, His primary method of creating meaning was through metaphor, simile, parable, and dramatic action rather than through logic and reasoning (very much the pedagogy of the Greeks, Hellenized Jews, and even the Romans). Therefore, when examined with care, Jesus's parables constitute serious but subtly disguised doctrine; and thus, He emerges as an extremely astute theologian.[2]

Why use metaphors and parables? Metaphors communicate in ways that rational arguments cannot. When used in theological settings to create meaning, parables specifically challenge listeners in ways that abstract statements cannot approach. Metaphors do more than explain meaning; they create meaning. A parable is an extended metaphor and, as such, is not merely a delivery system for ideas but a house in which listeners and readers are invited to take up residence and view the world through different windows of that house. Parables infuse energy and clarification into their abstract reflections. As such, they are modes of theological discourse to transmit hidden meanings.

As we study the life of Jesus Christ, we are encouraged to examine the human predicament through the lens created by the parable. Up through the twentieth century, there was a stream of scholarship that argued for a scenario of "one point per parable." However, current scholarly studies allow for the presences of several themes, especially if we adopt the perspective of having "taken up residence in a house." We look out on the world described in the parable through more than one window, giving us multiple perspectives. With this backdrop, let us take a fresh look at two of Christ's more prominent parables—namely, the parable of the good Samaritan and parable of the lost sheep.

The Parable of the Good Samaritan
(a.k.a., "Give me a list of who my neighbor is")

Because familiarity with this parable borders on being universal in the Christian world, recounting all the details is unnecessary. We recall that a certain lawyer (code name for a Pharisee) seeking to trap Jesus into responding with something in violation of the law of Moses and one of its 10,613 interpretations, which then would be construed as blasphemy. This trap was the question, "Who is my neighbor?" The Pharisee anticipated that Jesus would give him a proverbial list of people who qualified as neighbors, which might possibly include some folks who the Jews and the law of Moses did not consider to be "neighbors." Thus, Jesus would be caught in the trap of blasphemy. However, in keeping with Christ's frequent pattern of responding to inquiries with His own questions, the conversation preceding the presentation of the parable contains a dialogue of four key theological questions:

1. Lawyer = What shall I do to inherit eternal life?
2. Jesus = What is written in the law, and how do you read it?
3. Lawyer = Who is my neighbor?
4. Jesus = Which of the three travelers became a neighbor?

Let us analyze these questions by doing a deeper dive into this theological orthodoxy (what should I believe?) and orthopraxis (what am I supposed to do?) exchange between the Rabbi (meaning Teacher) and the Lawyer. The first inquiry was designed to trap Jesus by seeking to elicit a response that would be construed and twisted by His enemies, primarily the Pharisees, who perpetually looked for reasons that either Jesus's words or actions were blasphemous and therefore punishable by death under the strict interpretations of the law of Moses fostered by the Pharisees, or ultimately into a denial of the validity of the law of Moses. However, to the chagrin of the lawyer, Jesus perceives what the lawyer's intent is; so he turns the tables on him by seeking the lawyer's reaction to a related question (#2) and then using that response to answer the original question (#1).

However, the lawyer's original question (#1) is flawed. What can anyone do to *inherit* anything? An inheritance, by its very definition and nature, is a gift, especially when it comes to eternal life. It cannot be earned. Further, an inheritance is not a payment for services rendered or a reward for good works. It should be noted, in passing, that this kind of discussion (between Jesus and a Pharisee) regarding eternal life was commonplace among rabbis in the first and early second centuries. The lawyer summarizes his understanding of the Law—to "love your neighbor" (Leviticus 19:18) and to "love God" (Deuteronomy 6:5). One would have expected scripture quotes from the Old Testament to follow the canonical order, which is not how the lawyer structures his answer. Instead, we find "love God" is placed before the commandment to "love your neighbor." The order is important. Experience dictates that it is extremely hard to love the "unlovable" neighbor until a disciple's heart is filled first with the love of God, which then provides the motivation necessary for the arduous task of loving a "neighbor."

If acts of love are extended to others out of gratitude for the love of God, then a true disciple is sustained by the unwavering love of God toward him or her, regardless of the reaction of the neighbor to their acts of loving kindness, which could range from hostility to gratitude. In a complete turn of the tables, the lawyer finds himself on the horns of a dilemma. Processing knowledge of the Torah in his mind, the lawyer arrives at a logical conclusion:

> So, I must love God and my neighbor to inherit salvation. Fine, what I need now are a few definitions. To love God is to keep the law. I already know that. Second, what I need is clarification of exactly *who is* my neighbor, and *who is not* my neighbor. Once I have elucidation (i.e., a list) on this point, I can then proceed to successfully comply with the law.

Luke's rendition of the parable (see Luke 10:25–37) helps us understand further what is also going through the lawyer's mind by including, "He willing to justify himself, said unto Jesus, And who is my neighbour?" (Luke 10:29). Oops, wrong question, as we shall discuss below. To be justified is to be saved, and to be saved is to inherit eternal life. To be justified in biblical language means to be granted the status of one whom God accepts when he or she stands before Him at the judgment bar. The lawyer desires to justify himself clearly as a person who wants to achieve acceptance before God *on his own* through observance of the law. As a good first-century Jew, he expects Jesus to answer with a *list* of "neighbors" that the lawyer hopes he can manage. We can imagine the lawyer's list looking something like the following:

First, we have those who qualify as a neighbor:

- A "neighbor" automatically includes members of the Sanhedrin, regardless of their political maneuverings.

- A "neighbor" obviously includes a fellow Jew who keeps the law in precise fashion, for example, another Pharisee.
- A "neighbor" probably includes the Sadducees.
- A "neighbor" probably includes any regular, ordinary Jew not aligned with any particular faction of Judaism.
- A "neighbor" by divine edict must include "the stranger that dwelleth with you shall be unto you as one born among you, and thou shalt love him as thyself; for ye were strangers in the land of Egypt" (Leviticus 19:34).

Next, we have those who do not make the list of being a neighbor:

- A "neighbor" for sure will not include any Samaritan, because everyone knows that Yahweh hates the Samaritans. Hence, so does any upstanding Jew.
- A "neighbor" also would not include Essenes, who are the nutty Jews living on Masada having established their own version of Judaism.
- A "neighbor" does not include Zealots, who are fostering an agenda of revolution to rid the Holy Land of the Romans.
- A "neighbor" would certainly not include any pagans. Pretty much self-explanatory as to the reason why.
- Gentiles and pagans are not believers; and so, they clearly do not qualify as neighbors.

Probably on the proverbial bubble are the following:

- Jews who converted to Christianity.
- Perhaps, depending on the circumstances, a "neighbor" might be a proselyte—i.e., a gentile who converted to Judaism.

Hence, we now understand the lawyer's dilemma—he wanted a list of specifically who qualified and did not qualify as a "neighbor" so that he could be an observant Jew and measure his compliance with the law to be a good neighbor by acting in a neighborly fashion to whomever was a "neighbor" on the approved list. The tendency to read the law selectively was and continues to be an old problem. With a carefully drawn line between those who are and those who are not his neighbors, the lawyer would now be equipped to earn his way to eternal life—totally missing the point of eternal life being an inheritance which, again, cannot be earned.

Importantly, the lawyer's question, "Who is my neighbor?" is not answered. Instead, Jesus responds with a much larger and more significant conceptual and doctrinal framework, which is the real theological teaching of the parable: *"To whom must I become a neighbor?"* Christ's unique response being: Everyone. At great cost, the Samaritan became a neighbor to the wounded man. In the parable, the neighbor is the *Samaritan*, not the wounded man. Ibn-el-Tayyib, a Babylonian scholar circa AD 1025, provides insight:

> We see that the lawyer does not want to openly praise the Samaritan [for being a neighbor] and thus refers to him obliquely without naming him. This answer comes from his conscience, but he is fearful of Jewish attitudes [and social mores] with which he was raised. And if it were not for this parable *he would never concede that the Samaritan was a neighbor to the wounded man.*[3]

But the underlying and soul-stirring question remains unanswered, "Whose neighbor am I to become?" We are not told whether or not the lawyer "gets it" and realizes that having a list of people who are "qualified neighbors" does not satisfy the objective of bringing him to his desired goal of gaining eternal life. In sum, this magnificent parable teaches us that if we are to be beneficiaries of an inheritance of eternal life, we must answer the probing question, "To whom must I become a neighbor?" Then, having recognized that we are to be a neighbor to every child of God, we find ways to love them because we love God.

There is another dimension to this parable. We can examine it allegorically through the lens of a Latter-day Saint utilizing the light of the Restoration. The man who was going down is Adam, who is leaving Jerusalem (the Garden of Eden) intentionally, through his own volition. No one is forcing him to go down to Jericho. The reader should note that Jerusalem is 2,700 feet above sea level while Jericho is 825 feet below sea level. The destination called Jericho is mortality, a.k.a. the world. Adam believes that the journey is worth the risks of travel, which were well known to the people of Jesus's day. The robbers and thieves are the hosts of Satan who roam the earth. Adam, the man who is left "half dead," represents our fallenness and thereby becomes subject to the consequences of sin, which is tantamount to the first death. The Jewish priest, who happens by, which is not the result of chance, represents the law of Moses; the Levite represents the prophets, and the Samaritan (who is not from Judea) represents Christ (who is not of this world). The wounds are disobedience, which the Samaritan, having compassion, dresses with love, faith, and hope—the "ligatures" of salvation which cannot be undone. The bandages are the teachings of Christ, which bind us to righteousness. Oil represents the use of consecrated oil to heal the sick. The beast is the Lord's body. The inn (stable) which accepts all who wish to enter is the Church. The manager of the stable is the head of the Church, to whom its care has been entrusted. Payment for two days represents the time Christ spent in the tomb; and His promise to return on the third day alludes to His resurrection and paying (atoning) for all costs "whatever you expend." Finally, the declaration that the Samaritan promises to return represents the Second Coming.

In the light of the Restoration of God's plan of salvation, this parable packs compelling eternal mandates. Reading through a Christ-centered approach, we grasp the parable more fully as encouraging people to accept the Savior's atoning sacrifice by exhibiting love and mercy to their fellow beings. A Latter-day Saint construction using an allegorical methodology makes strong sense of each of the parable's elements. The pieces all interlock and fit together as they were designed to, thus illustrating how the scriptures truly testify of Christ.

The Parable of the Ninety and Nine
(a.k.a., The Lost Sheep)

No doubt that the Savior's parable of the lost sheep is one of the most loved and revered parables that Jesus taught His disciples. The reader will recall the circumstances surrounding the telling of the parable. Jesus has just taken Peter, James, and John to the Mount of Transfiguration. Following the sacred manifestations which occurred there, Jesus and the Twelve travel to Capernaum, where He teaches them about paying the temple tax, resolving the concern over who was the greatest among the Twelve, and identifying obstacles causing disciples to stumble, which issues specifically triggered Christ's saying, "Take heed that despise not one of these little ones" (Matthew 18:10). At that juncture, Christ recounts the parable of the lost sheep, which is presented below, highlighting three versions to enhance a deeper understanding.

King James Version	New Revised Standard Version	Wayment Translation
12. How think ye? If a man have an hundred sheep, and one of them be gone astray [or misled], doth not leave the ninety and nine, and goeth into the mountains, and seeketh that which is gone astray [misled]?	12. What do you think? If a shepherd has a hundred sheep, and one of them has gone astray, does he not leave the ninety-nine on the mountains and go in search of the one that went astray?	12. What do you think? If a certain person has a hundred sheep and one of them wanders off, does he not leave the ninety-nine in the mountains and search out the wandering sheep?
13. And if it so be that he find it, verily I say unto you, he rejoiceth more of that sheep, than of the ninety and nine which went not astray.	13. And if he finds it, truly I tell you, he rejoices over it more than over the ninety-nine that never went astray.	13. And if that person finds it truly, I say unto you that he will rejoice more over it than over the ninety-nine that did not wander.
14. Even so it is not the will of your Father which is in heaven, that one of these little ones should perish.	14. So it is not the will of your Father in heaven that one of these little ones should not be lost.	14. Therefore, it is the will of your Father in heaven that not one of these little ones be lost.

Some analysis and commentary would seem to be useful to share with you, the reader, at this point. St. Matthew identifies the shepherd as not being the owner of the sheep. They belong to the Father. Clearly, however, Jesus is the shepherd. The logic of the parable flows as follows: God (v. 14) approves of the actions of the shepherd Jesus who sets out to search for the lost sheep who has either gone astray or been misled. The Father is eager that none of "these little ones" might perish (vs. 13–14). Jesus describes himself as engaged in rescuing the lost. And those who believe in Jesus must do what He did. The disciples are addressed personally in the opening verse with the words, "Take heed that ye despise not one of these little ones" (Matthew 18:10). The message is clear—the Apostles are to search out any disciple who has strayed for whatever reason, as does the shepherd in the parable. What Jesus is already is doing, the Twelve are invited to do also.

It should further be noted that the reason for straying intentionally or absentmindedly, or in an alternative translation, being misled by someone or something, is irrelevant to initiating the shepherd's search. We all love this parable, even though we have read it or heard it taught in Sunday School and Primary classes or over the pulpit innumerable times. The message of rescuing the "one" resonates with true believers. However, this is a story about *costly love and risk*. A true story will set the foundation for my point.

At the end of World War II in 1945, Dr. Andrew Roy was serving in China as a professor for the Presbyterian Church. When the communists came to power in China in 1948, Dr. Roy opted to stay. After a few weeks of the new regime being in power, he was placed under house arrest, and then interrogated for two years before being allowed to leave. When describing the details of those interrogations, he emphasized how his communist inquisitors kept trying to convince him that the teachings of Jesus were vastly inferior to those of Karl Marx and Chairman Mao Zedong. Jesus's parable of the lost sheep was prominent in those interrogations. The communists insisted that to leave the ninety-nine and go after the one was irresponsible because the individual had value only as he or she contributes to "the people." According to the communist perspective, Jesus left the herd exposed to danger and thereby failed in his primary task. He irresponsibly risked the safety of 99 percent of the Father's herd.

Dr. Roy's answer was that the exact opposite was the case. By going after the *one*, Jesus conveyed to the ninety-nine a boundless security in that each one of them knew, "If I were to stray or be misled, the Shepherd would search for and rescue me." Failure to go after the one would leave those ninety-nine with the ultimate insecurity of realizing, "If I get lost or am misled, the shepherd will just leave me to die." Yes, there was risk involved, but deserved costly love was given to the one, thereby assuring it for the other ninety-nine. The greater the costly love expended, the greater the rejoicing if the lost is found and restored. Ah, but what about the ninety-nine? I believe that the message sent to the ninety-nine by the

Good Shepherd's actions is of equal importance in the plan as is the seeking out the one lost sheep. Last, the critical question is, does the rejoicing focus on the lost sheep or on the successful efforts of the searching shepherd? The shepherd says, "Rejoice with me for I have found the Father's lost sheep." The celebration is about the plan.

> "And if it so be that you should labor all your days in crying repentance unto this people [searching for and rescuing lost sheep], and bring, save it be one soul unto me, how great shall be your joy with him in the kingdom of my Father!" (D&C 18:15)

Jesus, the Good Shepherd, loved His Twelve Apostles, and indeed all His disciples. But just as there is a special reservoir of love for those who do not stray for whatever reason (i.e., the ninety-nine), there is great joy for those who are found and restored to the flock. Let there be no uncertainty about the intent of our Father in Heaven, who offers total approval of what the shepherd does to try and save all His sheep. The Father's will (and that of the shepherd) is for the sheep to heed His commandments, and unfailingly follow where Jesus the Shepherd leads. The fusion between the actions of the Good Shepherd and the desire of our Father in Heaven are of prime importance to the intent of the parable.

In all fairness, we should give equal billing to the one lost sheep. The following incident was shared with me by a long-time friend.

> Years ago, after the priesthood session of general conference, I [my friend] felt impressed to stop by Cheryl's [name changed for obvious reasons that become apparent below] apartment. I was eighteen years old at the time and felt a little awkward dropping by unannounced. However, my father had repeatedly counseled me as to the importance of following the promptings of the Holy Ghost, especially when they came as strongly as they did on this particular occasion. So, I acted on the whisperings of the Spirit. Cheryl, although taken aback when answering the door, invited me in. After we were seated, I began to describe my feelings with Cheryl about the wonderful priesthood session that I had just attended. In response to my invitation to share my notes with her,

she unhesitatingly agreed. Thus, I proceeded to summarize each of the remarks made by the Brethren who spoke.

As we spoke, her eyes filled with tears. Later, I learned that her boyfriend had called earlier in the day and invited her to be immoral with him later that evening. Cheryl had reluctantly agreed. As I spoke, the Spirit bore witness to her of the enormity of the transgression she was contemplating, and she resolved at that moment to never see this boyfriend again. Cheryl called him and cancelled the tryst.

Recently, I received a letter from Cheryl. She wrote in part, "I have since married a wonderful man in the temple and have five delightful children. I have frequently thanked my Heavenly Father for your visit that night so many years ago. By listening to what the Holy Ghost whispered for you to do—namely, visit me—you served as the instrument in the Lord's hands to help me prevent what would have been the most tragic mistake of my life. I can never repay you for what you did for me."

As members of the Church, we are in the rescuing business, now known as ministering. There are many sheep in need of being rescued. They need vitamins. Rescuing is about sending the unmistakable message of unconditional love and that none should be lost.

Notes

1. James Stevenson, ed., *A New Eusebius* (London: SPCK, 1957), 133, as quoted in Kenneth E. Bailey, *Jesus Through Middle Eastern Eyes* (Downers Grove, IL: InterVarsity Press, 2009), 277.
2. Adapted from Bailey, 279–83.
3. Ibn-al-Tayyib, *Sharah al-Mahriqi*, ed. Yusif Manqariyos, 2 vols. (Egypt: al-Tawfiq Press, 1907), 2:184. Note that this is an Arabic commentary on the Four Gospels by Abdullah Ibn al-Tayyib al-Mashriqi, originally composed in the eleventh century).

Chapter 7

Healing Physical and Spiritual Sickness

God is not merely seeking to heal us and thereby get us into heaven. He is seeking to get heaven into us.

Thoughtful study of the New Testament reveals that healing was a significant objective of the Savior's ministry. A closer look discloses that there were two types of healing involved in the scope of Christ's healing miracles: (1) healing of physical ailments, including diseases of all kinds, deformities, disabilities, etc., and (2) healing of spiritual sickness, primarily apostasy, which is tantamount to being on the wrong path to salvation by not embracing the "new" covenant heralded in the Messiah's fulfillment of the law of Moses (a.k.a., the "old" covenant). It should only require a sampling of verses found in the synoptic Gospels to remind us of Christ's innumerable miraculous acts of healing people physically. Consider the following (emphasis added):

> And Jesus went about all the cities and villages, teaching in their synagogues, and preaching the gospel of the kingdom, and *healing every sickness and every disease among the people.* (Matthew 9:35)

> And they departed, and went through the towns, preaching the gospel, and *healing everywhere.* (Luke 9:6)

> And Jesus went about all Galilee, teaching in their synagogues, and preaching the gospel of the kingdom, and *healing*

all manner of sickness and all manner of disease among the people. (Matthew 4:23)

And the people, when they knew it, followed him: and he received them, and spake unto them of the kingdom of God, and *healed them that had need of healing.* (Luke 9:11)

Given these and many more that could be quoted from the New Testament as well as from the Book of Mormon (which describes a plethora of healing blessings given by the Savior to those gathered at the temple in Bountiful), we have to ask ourselves the question, *Why?* The answer is found in understanding certain beliefs driving the cultural behavior of the Jews in the early first century AD, as well as the Nephites of Lehi's time in 600 BC, which arose from uninspired application of the law of Moses.

Jewish Laws of Purity

When Jesus was born in the meridian of time, there were essentially three major factions found in the practice of Judaism. The largest group who espoused one of the prevailing Jewish interpretations of the law of Moses was the Sadducees; the next largest group was the Pharisees; and finally, the Essenes. Although these three factions disagreed on multiple points of the law, they unanimously agreed concerning the "cleanliness" requirements to enter the temple and offer sacrifices (1) during High Holy Days (the Day of Atonement—we know it as Yom Kippur), (2) during observances of other festivals (Feast of Tabernacles, Feast of Unleavened Bread, Passover, and Feast of Weeks) throughout the year when the Jews were to make various sacrificial offerings, and (3) on Shabbat. Among those particularly onerous requirements was that, if a person was sick, disabled, blind, or had any other of a number of physical afflictions, then that person was prohibited from going to the temple and not allowed to worship as prescribed by the law of Moses because they were "unclean or impure."

However, the law did make allowances where leniency kicked in. Most of the circumstances which caused a Jew to be considered unclean were temporary. Once a person recovered from a disease or sickness or illness, they could go to the High Priest at the temple, be pronounced clean,

and were then able to enter the temple and participate in the ritual ceremonies required by the law. However, for blindness there was no allowance; it constituted a permanent ban from the temple because no one
in the history of Israel had ever been healed of blindness. Furthermore,
even in a scenario where the blind person had a spouse, child, brother, or
sister who could see and function as a guide, it was still not permitted for
the blind person to enter the temple even if accompanied by a guide. We
ask, "What was the basis for such strict rules precluding certain 'unclean'
individuals from worshipping in the temple?"

After Moses received the Ten Commandments on Sinai, Jewish
teachers and priests were asked innumerable questions about how the Ten
Commandments applied under various circumstances and situations—
for instance, defining "work" so as to avoid it on Shabbat. Over the course
of time, after the construction of the mobile tabernacle in the wilderness,
and again after the two permanent temples had been built in Jerusalem,
10,613 interpretations of the original Ten Commandments had been
adopted governing all aspects of daily Jewish life. These interpretations
became what is known as orthopraxis—what should I do to live the law.
Interpretations restricting those not permitted to worship at the temple
were based on a false notion—namely, that the reason people were sick,
had afflictions, disabilities, blindness, etc.—that either the person had
sinned or their parents had sinned (see discussion below). In sum, they
were unclean and were thus barred from entering and worshipping in the
temple. We see this manifest in the encounter that Jesus and the disciples
had with the man blind from birth. It is dismaying that the disciples sub-
scribed to that erroneous notion:

And as Jesus passed by, he saw a man which was blind from his
birth.

And his disciples asked him, saying, Master, *who did sin, this
man, or his parents,* that he was born blind?

Jesus answered, Neither hath this man sinned, nor his parents: but that the works of God should be made manifest in him.
(John 9:1–3; emphasis added)

We recall that Jesus had compassion on the blind man and healed
him. This miracle was stunning in several ways. First, Jesus healed

(considered work by Judaic definition) on Shabbat, which was strictly forbidden; second, no one could recall witnessing a person ever being healed of blindness. The Sadducees and Pharisees were not only livid about Jesus breaking the Sabbath, but also totally flabbergasted that blindness had been healed. So now, we inquire again. Why so much focus on healing? Jesus wanted all people, regardless of their circumstances, to be able to go to the temple and participate in the worship rituals and ceremonies not only during the Days of Atonement (Yom Kippur) and other periodic festivals such as Passover, Feast of the Tabernacles, etc., but also just to be able to present the weekly offerings on Shabbat. He also wanted people to know that physical ailments were not the result of sin.

The hope was that by observing the ritual sacrificial ordinances in the temple, the Jews would comprehend that the purpose of the law of Moses was to be a schoolmaster that would point them to Christ, and that the Jews would recognize Him as the Promised Messiah. Because of His unlimited and unconditional love, Jesus went about removing whatever man-made barriers that were hindering people from entering the temple. Some Jews in the Holy Land had rigorously observed the law of Moses and had figured out that the temple and sacrificial rituals pointed to Christ. So, when He walked among them in His mortal ministry, they accepted His message and became avid disciples. Sadly, many Jews did not get it. The Nephites, on the other hand, got it.

The Master's Touch

There is another dimension regarding the miraculous healing of physical ailments that deserves our attention.

> And, behold, there came a leper and worshipped him, saying, Lord, if thou wilt, thou canst make me clean.
>
> And Jesus put forth his hand, and touched him, saying, I will; be thou clean. And immediately his leprosy was cleansed. (Matthew 8:2–3)

Jesus could have cured the leper by just uttering words of healing. Was there really a need for Jesus to *touch* the leper? There was every need, for no one else would touch him. A healthy human hand was never laid on an unclean person in spite of the fact that the Jews had a ritual for healing that was the equivalent of our present-day anointing of oil—but everyone was afraid to touch leprous flesh. It made the toucher unclean or impure and therefore unworthy to enter the temple. Thus, lepers were despised and rejected within Jewish culture and community.

Although significant that Jesus healed the physical malady, He fed a greater need—comfort and peace for a sore, ailing heart. Of all men, the leper needed to be touched with the hand of love. It was not necessary for the Master to draw the leper around Him in the skirts of His garments and speak lofty words of healing so that this wretched creature might be at least clean *before* Jesus touched him. The man was a child of God, a brother, with a debilitating disease. Without hesitation, out went the divine Healer's loving hand to the ugly, diseased skin, and there miraculously and instantaneously, was His brother as he should be—standing purified with the flesh of a child.

I thank God that the touch preceded the words. Nor do I think, on the other hand (no pun intended), that it was merely the touch of a fingertip. It was a kindly, healing, consoling touch in its nature as well as its power. The insightful words of nineteenth-century cleric George MacDonald (mentor of C. S. Lewis) come to mind:

> Oh blessed leper! Thou knowest henceforth what kind of a God there is in the earth—not the God of the priests, but a God such as himself only can reveal to the hearts of his own. *That touch was more than the healing.* It was to the leper what the word *Daughter* was to the woman in the crowd, what the *Neither do I* was to the woman in the temple—the sign of the perfect presence.[1]

Our challenge as Latter-day Saints is to identify and respond appropriately to circumstances and situations where healing is the unmistakable manifestation of charity. As one non-LDS scholar concluded:

> Deification among the Latter-day Saints is . . . the progression and infinite multiplication of love.[2]

Healing Spiritual Sickness

Just as healing people from the seemingly innumerable types of physical ailments that were so prevalent in the first century, so was healing people from spiritual sickness. It is unfortunate that both Tyndale and the translation committees established by King James stuck with "hypocrite" and "hypocrisy" when transcribing *hypokrites* and *hypokrisis* from Greek to the English. Had they used "apostate" and "apostasy" instead, we in the twenty-first century would derive a totally different image of what Christ was depicting when he uttered *hypokrites* and *hypokrisis*. Given the unfortunate choice made by various translators, we miss why the Savior desired to heal the Sadducees and Pharisees. So, what was the spiritual affliction which drew the most attention from Jesus? Apostasy! And the apostates who inflicted it to varying degrees on those around them.

Hypocrisy, used in modern parlance, means the deliberate display and affectation of more virtue than one actually possesses. In our twenty-first-century minds, the word *hypocrisy* also suggests the outward display of piety, goodness, or sincerity when, in reality, a person is irreligious, corrupt, or insincere. The connotation is more than pretense—rather, it is the assumption of goodness and piety when one is neither good nor pious and does not want to be. As the reader probably knows or at least suspects, the word *hypocrisy* has Greek roots. The noun for it is *hypokrisis*, which is derived from the verb *hypokrinomai*, which means the dispensing of information. It was through the craft of *hypokrisis* (oral expression) that one could expound ideas with power. As such, hypocrisy was not just the art of selling an idea but of articulating it in a forceful manner. Thus, this is a totally appropriate characterization of the Pharisees as hypocrites. Flavius Josephus writings reveal that the Pharisees represented a reformist movement in Judaism attempting to arrogate themselves and their adherents a holiness belonging to the priesthood and trying to influence, at times even force, Jewish society to accept their particular interpretation of the scriptures.[3]

Furthermore, the Pharisees were able to convince many, even among the highest in Judean society, including the Sadducees, that righteousness and conduct pleasing to God could come only if they practiced the precepts of Mosaic law according to the rigid and strict Pharisaic interpretations.[4] Such interpretations greatly emphasized (1) the inerrancy of the Torah, particularly the book of Deuteronomy; (2) the strict observance of Shabbat, with almost two thousand "interpretations" of the definition of working and not working on the Sabbath; (3) temple worship, again with many rules to define "uncleanness" meant to preserve ritual purity; and (4) that salvation was "genealogical," meaning that only Abraham's posterity would be saved. One of the unintended consequences of oral expressions (hypocrisy) was to promulgate the practice of priestcraft since by the advent of Jesus, the Pharisees labored for money and honors of men. Hence, the disease which needed healing was a direct result of Pharisaic interpretation of the Scriptures and the practice of priestcraft which grew out of it. And what was this spiritual malady? Apostasy. Believing in falsehoods and propagating such incorrect beliefs to the people throughout Judea.

Note that in both the Old and New Testaments, there is no Hebrew or Aramaic equivalent to the Greek word *hypokrisis*. The Hebrew word that was translated into the Greek Old Testament (LXX—the Septuagint) and the Greek New Testament was *hanef,* which carries the ideas of (1) profaning, corrupting, or polluting, and (2) of being irreligious. Thus, *hypokrisis* was closely tied to the notion of standing in opposition to God. The *hypokrite* therefore was an ungodly man—an apostate. Deceit and lying are part of the bag of tools used to try and thwart God and lead His children away from the truth. In sum, *hypokrisis* reflects apostasy from God. No wonder Jesus wanted to heal the hypocrites. By performing miracles of healing, on the Sabbath no less, and in various sayings, He was hammering at the foundations of hypocrisy attempting to "heal" the apostate Pharisees and their followers from the spiritual myopia of apostasy. Forgiving sin was huge in this regard. And the coup de grâce was declaring Himself to be the Messiah. Jesus challenged every aspect of the misinterpretations of the law which the hypocrites preached and practiced concerning daily living, e.g., apostasy. He tried to open their eyes and lead them out of apostasy. Did it work? Some Pharisees did accept his message; however, sadly, many did not recover from the spiritual cancer of apostasy.

Ministering: Rescuing and Healing Today

Healing is about (1) learning "to whom must I become a neighbor" and (2) removing barriers preventing disciples from participating in ritual ordinances that point to and teach of Christ. Rescuing and healing further reflect the Savior's overarching love for all the children of Father in Heaven, regardless of their circumstances or situations while in this mortal probation. He set the example for us to follow. What a marvelous example was set for us by the Deliverer and the Redeemer to go about healing! Ministering sends the message to the "lost" disciple that we do not want any to be lost. Ministering sends the message to those who have not strayed that we will come in search of you should you find yourself lost in the mist of darkness. We know how to pass the tests of discipleship: to whom must I become a neighbor, and how can I become a resource to heal spiritual ailments?

Notes

1. George Macdonald, *The Miracles of our Lord* (London: Strahan & Co., 1870), 89; emphasis added.
2. M. David Litwa, *Becoming Divine: An Introduction to Deification in Western Culture* (Eugene, OR: Cascade Books, 2013), pp. 203–4.
3. See Ellis Rivkin, *A Hidden Revolution* (Nashville: Abingdon, 1978), 216–222.
4. See Josephus, *Antiquities* 13.5.289, where John Hyrcanus I, the high priest from 134 to 104 BC declared that their interpretation of the law showed one the true path of righteousness.

Chapter 8

"Believest thou the words which I shall speak?"

(Ether 3:11)

> The ability to . . . receive, and act on personal revelation is the single most important skill that can be acquired in this life.
>
> *(Julie B. Beck)*[1]

Along with many Latter-day Saints, I am intrigued by the journey of the families of Jared and his brother being led by the Lord to the same continent where He also directed the Nephites, which has been designated approximately fifty times in the scriptures as "a chosen land" (see Topical Guide, "Promised Lands"). Part of that fascination arises partly because of the name of the brother of Jared—Mahonri Moriancumer—but more importantly are all the parallels between the journeys traversed in the wilderness and crossing the sea. For purposes of the message of this chapter, I am assuming that the reader already has sufficient familiarity with the narrative found in the book of Ether in the Book of Mormon that it is not necessary to recite all the details here. Hence, I will provide only those portions of the Jaredite narrative which serve to illustrate my points.

The Jaredite adventure begins at the biblical tower of Babel. Languages are confused to frustrate the ill-conceived notion that man could build a tower high enough to climb into heaven, and to find the city of Enoch, as a bonus. Jared and his brother, along with their families and certain friends, are not confounded and are led away from the tower into the wilderness. They eventually end up at a seacoast, where they tarry for four years while the brother of Jared constructs, based on instruction provided by the Lord, eight vessels, which are used to transport the group safely to the land of promise. Upon completing the boat-building assignment, the brother of Jared realizes that, at certain times during the transversal process, there will need to be light inside the eight boats. After pondering this challenge, the brother of Jared decides that a viable solution is to fashion sixteen round stones and then ask the Lord to touch them, thereby causing them to glow and provide the needed light. He climbs the mountain again (for the umpteenth time) and presents his proposal to the Lord in prayer. Much to his astonishment, the Lord touches the stones with his finger.

Further on, during the sacred encounter with the Lord, there comes a most significant moment. The Lord asks a question, which is something which He often does when we approach him with our questions. If we "Hear Him" as President Russell M. Nelson has invited us to do in the April 2020 General Conference, especially when engaged in prayerful communion with our Father, we find that one manner of responding to our inquiries of Him, Father will ask us a question. In the case of Mahonri Moriancumer, the Lord asked a very striking question: "Believest thou the words which I *shall* speak [future tense]?" (Ether 3:11; emphasis added). Wait a minute! Unlike at the beginning of Nephi's vision wherein the angelic guide representing the Lord inquired, "Believest thou that thy father saw the tree of which he *hath* spoken [past tense]?" (1 Nephi 11:4), Mahonri was being asked to believe something that was yet to be revealed by God! Before the He begins, the Lord asks do you believe what I *shall* say—not will you believe after I have spoken, but do you believe it before I even tell you what it is that I am going to say? Such an inquiry takes faith to a whole new dimension. The Lord is saying, "Do you accept it before I say it?" I admit, at times, it can be challenging to believe what *has* been revealed. But to extend our faith to believe something that *shall* be revealed when we have no clue as to what sacred information might be presented is a whole other matter. Where is that bottle of vitamins?

Mahonri's response is powerful: "Yea, Lord, I know that thou speakest the truth, for thou are a God of truth, and canst not lie" (Ether 3:12).

What follows is a revelatory experience beyond the highest expectations the brother of Jared could have ever brought as a request to God. He received answers to questions he had not asked. That is what God does. At times, even when we ask the wrong or irrelevant questions, He responds with, "Well, here are the answers to the questions you should have asked." In sum, God asks for the past tense of belief (what He has said), or an assurance to accept and act even before the future tense (what He will say) of revealed truth.

Heavenly Wind

As frequent readers of the Book of Mormon, we recognize that it is packed with symbols intended to convey specific messages to us. One of those is the crossing of the sea—not just on a single occasion, but twice, in accordance with the law of witnesses. Both the Jaredites and the Lehites endured long passages (nearly a year in duration) across unknown and uncharted waters to a new land. The record tells us:

> The Lord God caused that there should be a *furious wind blow* upon the face of the waters, towards the promised land; and thus they [the Jaredites] were tossed upon the waves of the sea *before the wind.* (Ether 6:5; emphasis added)

> The Nephites also "put forth into the sea and were *driven forth before the wind* towards the promised land" (1 Nephi 18:8; emphasis added).

What was the nature of the wind upon the great waters? Examining the original Hebrew and Greek words which have been translated as "wind" reveals meaning which facilitates deeper understanding. In biblical text, the words for "wind" (Old Testament Hebrew *ruach* and New Testament Greek *pneuma*) mean "spirit" or "breath," and often refer to the presence of or activity of the Spirit of the Lord. Both the Jaredites and Nephites felt the forces of heavenly wind; they knew it came forth from the power of the Heavenly Spirit pushing them safely toward their divine destination.

And it came to pass that *the wind did never cease to blow* towards the promised land while they were upon the waters; and thus they were driven forth before the wind. (Ether 6:8; emphasis added)

Likening the scriptures to our lives, we have felt heavenly breezes blowing us along the covenant path. However, with the announcement that the Lord is hastening His work, the heavenly wind is ramping up to gale force. (Hence, buckle those seatbelts! And chow down some vitamins!) These winds will never cease to blow, driving us toward our eternal destiny and will not relent in their commission to deliver us back safely into the divine presence. I hasten to point out, not wanting to create feelings of anxiety or fear, that the existence of heavenly winds blowing in our lives are neither lesser nor greater than necessary to accomplish the objectives of the Lord's plan. Elder Richard G. Scott explained:

Just when all seems to be going right, challenges often come in multiple doses applied simultaneously. When those trials are not consequences of your disobedience, *they are evidence that the Lord feels you are prepared to grow more* (see Proverbs 3:11–12). He therefore gives you experiences that stimulate growth, understanding, and compassion which polish you for your everlasting benefit. To get you from where you are to where He wants you to be requires a lot of stretching, and that generally entails discomfort and pain. . . .

. . . Your Father in Heaven and His Beloved Son love you perfectly. *They would not require you to experience a moment more of difficulty [sailing in howling heavenly wind] than is absolutely needed for your personal benefit or for that of those you love.*[2]

How grateful we should be that heavenly winds are blowing us along the covenant path, and that we have an unending supply of vitamins to strengthen us during the journey. Brigham Young shared additional insight:

All intelligent beings who are crowned with crowns of glory, immortality, and eternal lives must pass through [blown by Heavenly Wind] every ordeal appointed for intelligent beings to pass through, to gain their glory and exaltation. . . . *Every trial and experience you have passed through is necessary for your salvation.*[3]

Yes, the Lord could have miraculously transported Jared's and Lehi's families across the sea to their destination in the land of promise without having them endure being driven by the winds which never ceased for nearly a year. But their journey, like ours, in mortality is specifically tailored to provide purifying preparation for greater things. May we be like those two courageous families; "They did cease not to praise the Lord" (Ether 6:9). "I know in whom I have trusted" (2 Nephi 4:20).

Fiery Furnaces

It is well for us to also remember that present and future trials, difficulties, and experiences of life each have a purpose and a blessing. Heavenly winds supplemented by "winds of adversity" can help us identify, reaffirm, and return to sound values and principles. They can make us more attentive to one another and help us to value relationships over things. They can deepen our spirituality and faith in God.

Recall the Old Testament account of Shadrach, Meshach, and Abednego who lived in captivity in Babylon during the reign of King Nebuchadnezzar who had sacked Jerusalem shortly after Lehi and his family had safely departed. These three faithful young men placed their trust in God when they refused to worship the king's golden idol. Even when threatened with being cast into the fiery furnace to be consumed in flames, they defiantly declared, "Our God whom we serve is able to deliver us from the burning fiery furnace. . . . *But if not*, be it known unto thee, O king, that we will not serve thy gods" (Daniel 3:17–18; emphasis added).

Two important understandings come to the forefront: (1) Shadrach, Meshach, and Abednego did *not* place their faith in anticipated or desired blessings; rather, their faith was constructed on the solid foundation in the Giver of blessings. (2) Their trust in God was not dependent on deliverance from the fiery furnace. They would go forward confidently, knowing that whatever might happen, they would be secure in God. In like manner, we should trust in the plan of salvation, its Author (the Father) and its Implementer, Jesus Christ. Elder Robert D. Hales warned us about fiery furnaces that will surely come. One Latter-day Saint scholar commented on Elder Hales's words:

> Elder Robert D. Hales taught, "In recent decades the Church has largely been spared the terrible misunderstandings experienced by the early Saints. *It will not always be so.*" Latter-day Saints have endured and will endure trials that will test their capacity to be "faithful in Christ" (Moroni 9:25). *These trials [fiery furnaces] may not come in the form of war and such extreme violence as depicted by Mormon*, but they will come, and the same tenacity with which Moroni remained faithful will be required to remain true. A faithful person has the ability to "Look unto [the Lord] in every thought; doubt not, fear not" (D&C 6:36). acknowledging that "The world is moving away from the Lord faster and farther than ever before. The adversary has been loosed upon the earth. We watch, hear, read, study, and share the words of the prophets to be forewarned and protected." The faithful are safeguarded by adherence to prophets' words and council, not only under every circumstance in a difficult world but in *every circumstance.*[4]

Having been forewarned, we should not be surprised by the unfolding of difficult daily events. Our trust in God will be our only sure and firm foundation. Check that seatbelt.

Heavenly Winds Disguised as Winds of Adversity

Sometimes we can feel that the heavenly winds are not favorable. Seemingly, they become winds of adversity in our minds when, in reality, they are heavenly winds with a different purpose. Consider the following true story:

> More than anything, Will wanted to be an Evangelist. He was only twenty-five, but he had already failed as an art dealer, language teacher, bookseller, and . . . been unsuccessful in love. However, more than all the paintings, all the words, all the

books, and all the women, Will wanted to devote himself to his fellow man and the Word of God as a minister of the Church. It was this passion that brought young Will to the coal fields of southern Belgium in the spring of 1879. It was here, in a tiny mining village, that Will overcame what he thought were winds of adversity in his life on the back of a faded envelope.

Perhaps it was the young minister's total selflessness that first captured the respect of the miners in that small community. When there was a mining disaster, scores of villagers were injured, and no one fought harder to save them than Will. Day and night, he nursed the wounded, fed the hungry, and clothed the poor. He even scraped slag heaps to provide townsfolk with fuel. After the rubble was cleared away, the dead buried, and the sick made well, the citizenry turned to Will who had healed their physical wounds and made him their spiritual leader. Every Sunday, the congregation filled Will's small chapel to overflowing to hear this unassuming man preach the Word of God. However, unexpectedly, and unannounced, the winds of adversity struck again.

A visiting Church official discovered Will living in a simple hut, dressed in an old soldier's coat, and wearing trousers made of sacking. When the cleric asked Will what he had done with his ministerial allowance, Will answered that he had given it to the miners and their families. The Church official told Will that he looked more miserable than the people to whom he was preaching. "Why had he given everything away?" stammered the Elder. Will simply responded, "Isn't that what Christ had intended for his disciples to do?" "Well, there's such a thing as too literally interpreting the scriptures," puffed the Church official. He went on in exasperation asserting that the "religious traditions" Will had dismantled would take years to rebuild. Will was dismissed from the service of the Church on the spot, that day. He was devastated. The career that had meant everything was gone. There followed months of despair. Then one afternoon, Will noticed an old miner, bending beneath the enormous weight of a full sack of coal. In that instant, Will felt again the desperation of these villagers . . . and recognized it would always be his own.

Fumbling through his pockets, he pulled out a tattered envelope, and then a pencil. . . . He began to sketch the weary figure that had moved him so. The first drawing was crude; but he repeated his artistic attempts again and again. Beginning that day, Will faced and eventually conquered the winds of adversity. Will captured for the world the torment, triumph, and dignity of the people he loved. If Will had failed as a minister, there was now a new passion and purpose. And, the villagers that he was no longer allowed to teach and inspire across the pulpit, he would reach through art. In the process, Will immortalized them . . . and they him. For the end of Will's career as a clergy man motivated a ministry more monumental than he had ever dreamed. Because the preacher who wasn't to be, became the artist the world would know as **Willem Vincent Van Gogh**.[5]

Truly, only the Savior can turn fiery furnaces and winds of adversity into heavenly blessings. Just as He stood with His three disciples through the flames, He stood with Van Gogh as he found another way to serve and reach the Belgian people whom he loved. The following lines are so reassuring:

May You Know

Enough happiness to keep you sweet,
enough trials to keep you strong;

Enough sorrow to keep you human,
enough hope to keep you happy;

Enough failure to keep you humble,
enough success to keep you eager;

Enough wealth to meet your needs, enough
enthusiasm to look forward;

Enough friends to give you comfort,
enough faith to banish depression;

Enough determination to make each day better than yesterday.[6]

Each of us has and will continue to be driven by heavenly winds (even though at time we may view them as winds of adversity) and will feel as though we have been blown into the fiery furnaces of circumstance. Further, there is no doubt that we will be called upon to believe words that are yet to be uttered by living prophets. Being firmly strapped in with our seatbelts, we will safely ride out the windy storms; and having taken our fire-resistance vitamins, we will endure any and all challenging situations that may come our way.

Notes

1. Julie B. Beck, "And Upon the Handmaids in Those Days Will I Pour Out My Spirit," *Ensign*, May 2010.
2. Richard G. Scott, "Trust in the Lord," *Ensign*, November 1995; emphasis added.
3. Brigham Young, in *Journal of Discourses*, 8:150; emphasis added.
4. Ezra Gwilliam, "Dear Son: Lessons from Moroni Chapter 9," *Religious Educator* 19, no. 1 (2015): 110. Gwilliam quotes Robert D. Hales, "General Conference: Strengthening Faith and Testimony," *Ensign*, November 2013.
5. Paul Aurandt, *Paul Harvey's Rest of the Story* (New York: Bantam Books, 1978).
6. Harold B. Lee, "Your Light to Be a Standard unto the Nations," *Ensign*, August 1973, 4.

Chapter 9

Which Way Do We Face?

"Be Thou My Vision"

Be thou my vision, O Lord of my heart . . .
Be thou my wisdom; be thou my true word,
Be thou ever with me, and I wish thee, Lord;
Be thou my great Father, and I thy true son [daughter];
Be thou in my dwelling, and I with thee one.
Be thou my breastplate, my sword for the fight,
Be thou my whole armor, be thou my true might.
Be thou my soul's shelter, be thou my strong tower
Oh raise thou me heavenward, great Power of my power.
High King of heaven, thou heaven's bright sun,
O, grant me its joys after the victory is won;
Great heart of my own heart, whatever befall,
Still be thou my vision, O Ruler of all

(Medieval Christian Hymn)[1]

Trying to please others *before* pleasing God is inverting the first and second great commandments (Matthew 22:37–39). It is forgetting which way we face. Through the prophet Isaiah the Lord warns us, "Fear ye not the reproach of men" (Isaiah 51:7). Decisions of courage, which is one of the pillars of a noble and Christlike character, are made by remembering the right order of the two great commandments. C. S. Lewis observed, "Courage is not simply one of the virtues, but the form of every virtue at the testing point. . . . Pilate was merciful till it became risky."[2] King Herod was reluctant at the request to behead John the Baptist but wanted to please "them which sat with him at meat" (Matthew 14:9). King Saul disobeyed the word of the Lord by keeping the spoils of war because he "feared the people and obeyed their voice" (1 Samuel 15:24). Many New Testament priests and chief rulers "believed on [the Lord]; but because of the Pharisees they did not confess him, lest they should be put out of the synagogue: For they loved the praise of men more than the praise of God" (John 12:42–43). Pilate, King Herod, King Saul, and the Pharisees didn't take their vitamins, so when the time came when it became necessary to take a stand and be true to God, they caved.

Follow the Prophet

Today, there are those who scornfully accuse the prophets of not living in the twenty-first century or of being bigoted. Such individuals and groups attempt to persuade or even pressure the Brethren to modify the Church by lowering standards, doctrines, policies to the level of their own inappropriate beliefs or behaviors. Elder Neal A. Maxwell said such situations "develop self-contentment instead of seeking self-improvement."[3] As humble and valiant disciples we should "never forget which way [we] face."[4] It does not do much good to be buckled up in a seatbelt facing the wrong direction or to be in the wrong vehicle going in the wrong direction.

President Spencer W. Kimball, while presiding at the Johannesburg South Africa Stake Conference held in December 1973, made the following statement that has been a beacon for me ever since: *"If we will just follow the Lord's prophets, we will arrive where they are going"* (emphasis added). Think about that! What an incredible statement! Think of the confidence, hope, and blessed assurance embedded therein! Over the years, I have been frustrated and disheartened when I hear people say, "I hope I will make it to the celestial kingdom." The answer is simple— follow the prophets and, most assuredly, we will arrive at where they are going. Prophets know what is around the next corner and over the next mountain along the covenant path. Astounding! Couple that with the inspired statement made by Paul to the Corinthians to help them understand the value of having living prophets:

> While we [Paul and the Twelve Apostles] look not at things which are seen, *but at the things which are not seen*: for the things

which are seen are temporal; *but the things which are not seen [by you and me] are eternal.* (2 Corinthians 4:18; emphasis added)

Seers are prophets who see what the rest of us cannot see.

I am reminded of the Old Testament story of Elisha the Prophet as recorded in 2 Kings 6. Recall that Syria was a constant thorn in Israel's side. After several repeated attempts to conquer the Kingdom of Israel, King Benhadad and his army came up to war against Israel one more time. However, when Benhadad set up camp for his army, Jehovah told Elisha the location of the camp, who in turn passed that strategic information along to King Jehoram (approx. 870 BC). No matter where the Syrian army camped, their encampment was successfully attacked by Israel's army. After several victories that decimated Syrian military installations, Benhadad became suspicious that there might be a traitor in his own camp who had betrayed their location to Israel's soldiers. Upon inquiring of his servants as to who the traitor might be, they said, "It is none of us; but it is Elisha the Prophet. Elisha knows everything. He is able to tell Jehoram the words you speak in your bedchamber." In a rage, Benhadad demanded that they find where Elisha was so he could deal with him. The fearful servants were able to locate Elisha in Dothan. As would be expected, Benhadad was deadly serious about eliminating Elisha. He sent horses, chariots, and a great army to surround Dothan at night. When Elisha's servant arose in the morning and saw the Syrian soldiers surrounding them, he was filled with fear, woke Elisha, and asked, "What shall we do?" Elisha replied, "Do not be afraid. Those who are with us are more than those who are with them." Then Elisha prayed, saying, "Lord, I pray thee, open his eyes, that he may see." (2 Kings 6:17). And when the eyes of the young servant were opened, he saw that the mountain was filled with horses and with chariots of fire all around Elisha. Seeing may be just as important as hearing. And if we add understanding, we have the perfect trifecta!

To provide a couple of additional examples, consider Noah, Nephi, and the brother of Jared who were called of God to build boats, of all things. What do we learn from arks and boats and barges constructed by prophets? Ponder the following observations:

- Don't miss the boat (particularly Noah's ark).
- We are all in the same boat (proverbially).
- Plan ahead—it wasn't raining when Noah constructed the ark.
- Stay fit. When you are six hundred years old, you may be asked to do something big.
- Don't listen to the critics and naysayers.
- Travel in pairs.
- Speed isn't always an advantage—snails were on board with the cheetahs.
- When stressed, float a while.
- Noah's Ark, Nephi's ship, and the brother of Jared's barges were built by amateurs. The Titanic was built by professionals.

In contrast, consider certain aspects of an idea proposed by a King but not sanctioned by a prophet; namely, to build a tower to heaven.

- It was hedging their bet on Noah's statement that there would not be another flood.
- We can sin without impunity.
- Let's make a name for ourselves (fame).
- Let's find another way to heaven, other than by following the plan and the prophets.

And the list goes on. It is not too difficult to figure out that arks, ships, and boats constructed by those who are taught by God are safer places of refuge than a tower built by an uninspired leader with unrighteous motives.

In the parable of the rich man and poor Lazarus, the Savior seems to be issuing a warning about caring for the poor and the urgent need to repent if indigent persons are being neglected. But the "punch line" is about listening to prophets.

There was a certain rich man, which was clothed in purple and fine linen, and fared sumptuously every day:

And there was a certain beggar named Lazarus, which was laid at his gate, full of sores,

And desiring to be fed with the crumbs which fell from the rich man's table: moreover the dogs came and licked his sores.

And it came to pass, that the beggar died, and was carried by the angels into Abraham's bosom: the rich man also died, and was buried;

And in hell he lift up his eyes, being in torments, and seeth Abraham afar off, and Lazarus in his bosom.

And he cried and said, Father Abraham, have mercy on me, and send Lazarus, that he may dip the tip of his finger in water, and cool my tongue; for I am tormented in this flame.

But Abraham said, Son, remember that thou in thy lifetime receivedst thy good things, and likewise Lazarus evil things: but now he is comforted, and thou art tormented.

And beside all this, between us and you there is a great gulf fixed: so that they which would pass from hence to you cannot; neither can they pass to us, that would come from thence.

Then he said, I pray thee therefore, father, that thou wouldest send him to my father's house:

For I have five brethren; that he may testify unto them, lest they also come into this place of torment.

Abraham saith unto him, They have Moses and the prophets; *let them hear them.*

And he said, Nay, father Abraham: but if one went unto them from the dead, they will repent.

And he said unto him, *If they hear not Moses and the prophets, neither will they be persuaded, though one rose from the dead.* (Luke 16:19–31; emphasis added)

How blessed we are to not only have a plethora of ancient prophets whose recorded words are readily available to study and ponder but also the declarations of living prophets, which include interpretations of what the former-day prophets wrote about. Listening to and following the prophets will not only get us to where they are going but also keep us in the kingdom (facing the right direction) which we entered by descending into the waters of baptism during our sojourn here in mortality.

"Listing"

Mormon, one of the authors and editors of the Book of Mormon, summarizes the circumstances surrounding Alma 1 and the Amlicites in their continuing wars and contentions, which occurred in the fifth year of the reign of the judges.

> And in one year were thousands and tens of thousands of souls sent to the eternal world, that they might reap their rewards according to their works, whether they were good or whether they were bad, to reap eternal happiness or eternal misery, *according to the spirit which they LISTED to obey, whether it be a good spirit or a bad one.*
>
> *For every man [or woman] receiveth wages of him whom he LISTETH to obey.* (Alma 3:26–27; emphasis added)

"List" is a word not heard nor read in common usage today. Its definitions include "to incline," "to bend toward," "to tilt," or "to be leaning away from upright." We encounter the use of this word in the Old Testament book of Amos when the prophet has an interesting conversation with Yahweh:

> The Lord stood upon a wall made by a plumbline, with a plumb line in his hand.
>
> And the Lord said unto me, Amos, what seest thou? And I said, A plumbline. Then said the Lord, Behold, I will set a plumbline in the midst of my people Israel: I will not again pass by them any more [referring to Passover when the angels of death passed by those children of Israel who had painted their door posts with blood; and meaning that the Lord will no longer ignore their transgressions]. (Amos 7:7–8)

The purpose of a plumb line (a device still used in construction today) is to determine whether a wall is improperly bending, inclining, or tilting—that is, *listing*. God told Amos that he meant to measure Israel with a plumb line to see if there were any guilty of the thing which King Benjamin warned his people about—listing away from the straight and narrow path: "Beware lest . . . ye *list* to obey the evil spirit" (Mosiah 2:32).

Listing is not the same as "open rebellion"; rather it is a subtle drifting, slight inclination, or nearly invisible attraction toward the enticements of sin and away from the straight and narrow path that might go unnoticed without using a plumb line. Uncorrected, a wall that is listing will eventually collapse.

John Donne reached the pinnacle of ministerial success, becoming the dean of St. Paul's Cathedral (in London) and preaching regularly before King Charles I and the royal family. Almost totally neglected for more than three hundred years before being discovered a century or so ago, John Donne returns from his grave to give us a final word of confidence as we make our way along the covenant path. Our friend and English preacher said this:

> We ask our daily bread, and God never says you should have come yesterday. He never says [I have run out] you must come again tomorrow, but today if ye will *hear His voice,* today He will hear you. . . . He brought light out of darkness, not out of a lesser light; He can bring summer out of winter, though thou have no spring; though in the ways of fortune, or understanding, or conscience, thou have been benighted till now, wintred and frozen, clouded and eclipsed, damp and benumbed, smothered and stupefied till now, now God comes to thee, not as in the dawning of the day, not as in the bud of the spring, but as the sun at noon, to illustrate all shadows, as the sheaves in harvest, to fill all penuries, all occasions invite His mercies, and all times are His seasons.[5]

Safety and certainty of direction as we move through life come from listing toward and hearing the prophets. Furthermore, we will find ourselves facing the right way.

Aligning Our Will to His

Elder Maxwell describes how the blessings of happiness can be opened to us:

> Petitioning in prayer has taught me that the vault of heaven, with all its blessings, is to be opened only by a combination lock: one

tumbler falls when there is faith, a second when there is personal righteousness, and the third, and final tumbler falls only *when what is sought is (in God's judgment—not ours) "right" for us.* Sometimes we pound on the vault door for something we want very much, in faith, in reasonable righteousness, and wonder why the door does not open. We would be very spoiled children if that vault door opened any more easily than it now does. I can tell, looking back, that *God truly loves me by the petitions that, in his perfect wisdom and love, He has refused to grant me. Our rejected petitions tell us not only much about ourselves, but also much about our flawless Father.*[6]

Ponder for a moment that the wrestle Enos had before God was really with himself (see Enos 1:2). Often the greatest effort is put forth when a person contends with himself or herself before the Lord. Such wrestling is the struggle to discover, admit, and express one's real desires, which can, at times, be hidden behind sin, evasion, guilt, and cover-up. Wrestling with oneself involves deep thought, meditation, and concentration. It means going beyond the cliché level of prayer to the point where we truly pour out our souls and prepare room for God to pour in.

Repetitions cease to be vain, trite, or insincere. Instead, each phrase becomes an expression of a yearning desire to do God's will. Such prayers are guided by the Holy Ghost: "For we know not what we should pray for as we ought; but the Spirit itself maketh intercession for us with groanings which cannot be uttered" (Romans 8:26). Enos's choice of words, which were guided by the Holy Ghost, in verses three and four—"sunk deep," "hungered," "cried," "mighty prayer and supplication," "raise my voice high"—effectively demonstrate his efforts to truly communicate with his Father in Heaven, a perfect example for us. C. S. Lewis provides a capstone to the topics discussed herein:

What Satan put into the heads of our remote ancestors was the idea that they could be like gods—they would set up on their own as if they had created themselves—to be their own masters—*invent some sort of happiness for themselves outside God, apart from God.* And out of that hopeless attempt has come nearly all that we call human history—money, poverty, ambition, war, prostitution, classes, empires, slavery—*the long terrible story of man [or woman] trying to find something other than God which will make him happy.*

That is the key to history. Terrific energy is expended—civilizations are built up—excellent institutions are devised; but each time something goes wrong. Some fatal flaw always brings the selfish and cruel people to the top and it all slides back into misery and ruin. In fact, the machine conks. It seems to start up all right and runs a few yards, and then it breaks down. *They are trying to run it on the wrong juice. This is what Satan has done to us humans.*[7]

In sum, being buckled in facing the wrong direction is just a precarious as taking the wrong vitamins and expecting the energy derived therefrom to be productive.

Waiting on the Lord

Another perspective concerning "which way do you face" is that our patience could wear thin. Consequently, we do one of two things: (1) we turn and face the wrong direction, or (2) we simply walk away from facing the right direction. Elder Maxwell encourages us to be patient, which, among other things, exhibits our willingness to submit to His will, including timing. Waiting could also involve being tempted by distractions, such as "the cares of the world," which is what happened to James Covel, who after serving as a Baptist minister for more than forty years had joined the young Church in Fayette, New York (see D&C 39:9 and 40:2). Elder Maxwell teaches:

> Patience is not indifference. Actually, it means caring very much but being willing, nevertheless, to submit to the Lord and to what the scriptures call the *"process of time."*
>
> Patience is tied very closely to faith [trust] in our Heavenly Father. Actually, when we are unduly *impatient* we are suggesting that we know what is best—better than does God. Or, at least, we are asserting that our timetable is better [more inspired] than His. . . .

We read in Mosiah about how the Lord simultaneously tries the patience of His people even as he tries their faith (Mosiah 23:21). One is not only to endure, but to endure well and gracefully those things which the Lord "seeth fit to inflict upon [us]" (Mosiah 3:19), just as did a group of ancient American saints who were bearing unusual burdens but who submitted "cheerfully and with patience to all the will of the Lord" (Mosiah 24:15). . . .

. . . Sometimes that which we are doing is correct enough but simply needs to be persisted in patiently, not for a minute or a moment but sometimes for years. . . .

. . . Patience is a willingness, in a sense, to watch the unfolding purposes of God with a sense of wonder and awe, rather than pacing up and down within the cell of our circumstance. Put another way, too much anxious opening of the oven door and the cake falls instead of rising. So it is with us. If we are always selfishly taking our temperature to see if we are happy, we will not be.

. . . Whereas faith and patience are companions, so are selfishness and impatience. . . .

Patience is, therefore, clearly not fatalistic, shoulder-shrugging resignation. It is acceptance of a divine rhythm to life; it is obedience prolonged. Patience stoutly resists pulling up the daisies to see how the roots are doing.[8]

Waiting on the Lord involves trusting in the timing of God's plan. When we become impatient, we are literally saying that our time frame is better than Father's—a dangerous place to be! On occasion, my wife gently reminds me to take my "patience" vitamins. Another dimension of waiting is that some of the testing and proving that God has designed individually for you and me is that the process is not instantaneous. We have become accustomed to the twenty-minute-sitcom world where every situation is resolved. Eternal development will take longer than we expect or want. Patience is a key ingredient in the recipe of repentance and growth. It may seem inconsistent and almost paradoxical with the hastening of the work and the shortening of the time prior to the Second Coming that we are to exercise patience. It would be more logical that we should be anxiously engaged at a greater rate of speed. But "waiting on the Lord" has not been rescinded. I am reminded of the counsel of President Harold B. Lee:

> There will be some things that take patience and faith. You may not like what comes from the authority of the Church. It may contradict your political views. It may contradict your social views. It may interfere with some of your social life. But if you listen to these things, as if from the mouth of the Lord himself, with patience and faith, the promise is that "the gates of hell shall not prevail against you; yea, and the Lord God will disperse the powers of darkness from before you, and cause the heavens to shake for your good, and his name's glory" (D&C 21:6).[9]

There is another dimension of the danger of being impatient. In the scriptures, the word *rest* is found fifty-eight times. *Rest* can also be defined/translated as "remainder." It appears that one of the purposes of Sabbath "resting" is to enable the Lord to provide us with continuing personal revelation regarding the "remainder" of the Restoration of the gospel. Impatience would preclude us from taking the time to empty out the things of the world that do not matter, so that we have room for the "remainder" of the fulness of the gospel. President Joseph F. Smith taught:

> In coming here, we forgot all, that our agency might be free indeed, to choose good or evil, that we might merit the reward of our own choice and conduct. But by the power of the Spirit, in the redemption of Christ, through obedience, *we often catch a spark from the awakened memories of the immortal soul,* which lights up our whole being as with the glory of our former home.[10]

We do not arrive in mortality with a blank slate, although I am sadly aware of members of the Church who believe that false idea. In the premortal existence, we were engaged in a very intense training program of unknown length; we fought in a war of conflicting ideas about how to become like our Heavenly Parents, which is still going on today. All those premortal experiences, virtually all of which we have temporarily forgotten, had a significant impact on our souls. We do not know how all these events that occurred in the world of spirits determined the timing, geographical location, and family line with which we would enter mortality to begin our education here on earth. But we came "trailing clouds of glory" and armed with knowledge learned in our premortal school.

Notes

1. As quoted in Susan W. Tanner, "Faith in Jesus Christ," Religious Educator 20, no. 2 (2019): 50.
2. C. S. Lewis, *The Screwtape Letters*, rev. ed. (New York: Macmillan, 1982), 137–38.
3. Neal A. Maxwell, "Repentance," *Ensign*, November 1991.
4. Lynn G. Robbins, "Which Way Do You Face?" *Ensign*, November 2014.
5. John Donne, "Sermon II. Preached on Christmas Eve, 1624," as quoted in *The Works of John Donne: With a Memoir of His Life,* ed. Henry Alford (London: John W. Parker, 1839), 1:25.
6. Neal A. Maxwell, "Insights from My Life" (Brigham Young University devotional, October 26, 1976), speeches.byu.edu; emphasis added.
7. C. S. Lewis, *Mere Christianity* (New York: Macmillan, 1958), 39.
8. Neal A. Maxwell, "Patience" (Brigham Young University devotional, November 27, 1979), speeches.byu.edu.
9. Harold B. Lee, in Conference Report, October 1970.
10. Joseph F. Smith, *Gospel Doctrine* (Salt Lake City: Deseret Book, 1939), 13–14; emphasis added.

Chapter 10

Prayer and Gifts of the Spirit

Prayer is the soul's sincere desire, uttered or unexpressed.
("Prayer Is the Soul's Sincere Desire," Hymns, no. 145)

As discussed in chapter 1 of this book, 2020 was designated as a year to celebrate and do a deeper dive into the events surrounding the First Vision, the coming forth of the Book of Mormon, the angelic bestowal of priesthood keys, the initiation of the Restoration of the Church, and the unfolding of the fulness of the gospel, a process which is continuing today, two hundred years later. We are reminded that the foundations of the restored Church of Jesus Christ of Latter-day Saints are anchored in prayer. It was, as we know, the fervent prayer of young Joseph Smith which opened the door to the grand process of continuing revelation, over the course of time, of the fulness of the gospel of Jesus Christ. We recall the words in James 1:5, "If any of you lack wisdom, let him ask of God," which had such a powerful impact on the about-to-be-called prophet. Yet, sometimes, we do not continue to read the ensuing two verses, which say: "But let him ask in faith, nothing wavering. . . . For let not that man [that is, the man who wavers] think that he shall receive any thing of the Lord" (James 1:6–7). We cannot expect answers when we are wavering in the winds of doubt.

An Overlooked Dynamic of Prayer

In addition to this seminal scripture, which contains the key to unlocking the treasure house of God's knowledge and wisdom, there are others which further define the principle of prayer and its application in our lives. For example, Amulek teaches us: "Yea, and when you do not cry out unto the Lord [in vocal prayer], let your hearts be full, drawn out in [non-vocal] prayer unto him continually for your welfare" (Alma 34:27). It is clear then, when we are not actually engaged in the formal act of vocal prayer, we should always have a non-vocal prayer in our hearts, wherever we are or whatever we are doing. Another key scripture takes prayer beyond being merely an admonition and into the realm of being a commandment:

> And again, I command thee that thou shalt pray vocally as well as in thy heart; yea, *before the world as well as in secret, in public as well as in private.* (D&C 19:28; emphasis added)

We may ask, "Why has God seen fit to make it a commandment that we pray both vocally and in secret (meaning non-vocally)?" Obviously, secret prayer is necessary in many situations where it would be awkward or unfeasible to pray vocally. But a more significant reason for praying non-vocally has been revealed by God:

> Yea, I tell thee, that thou mayest know that there is *none else save God that knowest the thoughts and the intents of thy heart.* (D&C 6:16, emphasis added)

It is more than comforting to know that Satan and his minions, who were cast out of God's presence, are dead to His Spirit, and are thereby excluded from the thoughts and intents of our hearts while in engaged in secret (non-vocal) prayer. Thus, in His infinite wisdom, love, and mercy, God has provided a channel of communication between Himself and His children here on earth that Satan, our common and relentless enemy, cannot invade. This is the channel of secret, non-vocal, prayer. The significance of this to Latter-day Saints is profound, for by such means we communicate with our Heavenly Father in sacred secrecy, confident that the adversary cannot intrude. We remember of the words of a favorite hymn:

Secret Prayer

There is an hour of peace and rest,
unmarred by earthly care;
'Tis when before the Lord I go
and kneel in secret prayer.

The straight and narrow way to heav'n,
where angels bright and fair
Are singing to God's praise, is found
through constant secret prayer.

When sailing on life's stormy sea,
'mid billows of despair,
'Tis solace to my soul to know
God hears my secret prayer.

When thorns are strewn along my path,
and foes my feet ensnare,
My Savior to my aid will come,
if sought in secret prayer.

Chorus
May my heart be turned to pray,
pray in secret day by day
That this boon to mortals giv'n may
unite my soul with heav'n.

(*Hymns*, no.144; emphasis added)

The Prophet Joseph Smith taught that "some revelations are of God; some revelations are of man; and some revelations are of the devil."[1] While Satan can and often does convey thoughts, he does not know whether these thoughts have taken root unless they are reflected either in our vocal prayers or in our outward actions. Hence, the powerful counsel offered by Paul:

> For we know not what we should pray for as we ought: but the Spirit itself maketh intercession for us with *groanings which cannot be uttered.* (Romans 8:26)

More often than not, secret non-vocal prayers become the source of learning what it is that we are to pray for vocally (personal revelation).

We should, of course, offer inspired vocal prayers (family prayers, baby naming, father's blessings given to children at least annually, and prayers in various Church meetings, etc.), the content of which is whispered to us by the Holy Ghost. But how much more important is it to listen for personal revelation when we pray in secret, and then preciously guard those silent utterances, thus precluding Satan from wedging his way into our lives to try and deceive us?

True Prayer Is Worship

In what I hope will be received in a spirit of love, may I suggest a couple of examples of what a prayer of faith might look like.

- First, a "good prayer": Heavenly Father help me feel better about myself.
- Second, a "better prayer": Heavenly Father help me feel better about myself: "Nevertheless, thy will be done."
- Third, an "even better prayer": Heavenly Father, I know that you love me. And I know you are anxious for me to feel better about myself. And I am so grateful for the spiritual gifts you have already given me to help me feel better about myself. And if there is something I should be praying for, please help me know what it is. (See Romans 8:26, quoted above.)

To some of you, praying for what you already know that God knows that you need can be a bit challenging and confusing. But here's a thought from Chauncey Riddle, PhD, BYU Emeritus Professor of Philosophy, who wrote: "It may seem strange that in certain prayers one might simply repeat what he [or she] is given to say by the Holy Spirit unless one realizes that *true prayer is worship*.[2] Adding to this thought, Elder Bruce R. McConkie wrote: *"Perfect prayers are spoken by the power of revelation."*[3] When our prayers are inspired, we learn from our petitions to our heavenly home. To be able to tap into divine perspective regarding the content of our prayers becomes increasingly important. There is only one way in which we are guided in the content of our prayers. We must come to bend our will to the will of God, so that in our prayers we really commune with Him and thereby ask for those things that are right, which includes supplicating for gifts of the Spirit.

Gifts of the Spirit

It is no accident that gifts of the Spirit are enumerated three times in the scriptures—namely, 1 Corinthians 12, Doctrine and Covenants 46, and Moroni 10. Such listings were directed to Paul, Joseph Smith, and Moroni in full accordance with the law of witnesses. I hasten to point out, however, that these three enumerations are meant to be illustrative, not comprehensive. Indeed, as Elder Bruce R. McConkie has affirmed, *"In the fullest sense, spiritual gifts are infinite in number and endless in their manifestations."*[4] The Apostle Paul encouraged the first-century saints, "Even so ye, forasmuch as ye are zealous of spiritual gifts, *seek that ye may excel to the edifying of the church*" (1 Corinthians 14:12; emphasis added). By inviting *all* saints to anxiously pursue gifts of the Spirit, Paul rejected the theology of "spiritual elitism" as God's method of allocating spiritual gifts. Paul sought to educate the saints about the need and appropriateness petition God for various gifts promised to all worthy saints, not just a small group of what some perceive as the "in crowd." Hugh Nibley provides necessary and important insight:

> The gifts [of the Spirit] are spiritual. . . . *We can't conjure them up for ourselves. The Lord gives them*, and He says He gives them in response to our petitioning for them. We must ask for them with real intent and with an honest heart. We have them—*any gift . . . all these things are available—all we need is to ask.* But we must *ask* for them, and of course if we ask not, we receive not.[5]

Gifts of the Spirit are essential vitamins. Paul identifies Heavenly Father as the origin from which all gifts derive their existence (see 1 Corinthians 12:6); consequently, it is God who determines to whom each gift is entrusted, "as it hath pleased him" (1 Corinthians 12:18). They are abundant and readily available to those who seek them in humble prayer.

I have often wondered why the gifts of the Spirit recounted in verses 8–19 found in Moroni 10 are almost verbatim when compared to Paul's list found in 1 Corinthians 12, especially since they are recorded by Moroni right after his promise on how to know if the Book of Mormon is true as contained in verses 3–5. After much pondering, I realized that what Moroni was telling us is that the manifestation of any of the gifts of the Spirit in our lives is tantamount to receiving a testimony that the Book of Mormon is true. The Holy Ghost is witnessing that the Book of Mormon is true through gifts of the Spirit. Unfortunately, many people tend to believe that the reception of a testimony of the truthfulness of the Book of Mormon must always come in one specific type of spiritual manifestation from the Holy Ghost. Such a notion is just not true. The Holy Ghost has many gifts by which He can be the testator/revealer/confirmer of truth.

Paul's counsel to his close missionary associate, Timothy, is also applicable to us: "Neglect not the gift that is in thee" (1 Timothy 4:14). It is not only prudent but also wise that we do not put at risk our inheritance of spiritual gifts either through disregard or apathy. High on the list of indictments that might be leveled against an unwise steward is that of either rejecting or not utilizing the very gifts conferred according to the design of God. We would do well to heed the words of Flavius Magnus Aurelius:

He is invited to do great things who receives small things greatly.[6]

Having alluded to gifts of the Spirit as essential vitamins, in another sense, they could also be viewed as seatbelts that keep us on the covenant path. The departure of spiritual gifts was one of the casualties of the great apostasy. Two biblical scholars have noted:

Concerning these [spiritual gifts], our whole information must be derived from Scripture, because they seem to have vanished with the disappearance of the Apostles themselves, and there is no authentic account of their existence in the Church in any writings of a later date than the books of the New Testament.[7]

Further acknowledgment of the loss of spiritual gifts that preceded the great apostasy was made by John Wesley, who lamented:

It does not appear that these extraordinary gifts of the Holy Spirit were common in the Church for more than two or three centuries. We seldom hear of them after that fatal period when the Emperor Constantine declared himself a Christian.[8]

The Restoration of the Lord's gospel and church included the revival of spiritual gifts which had remained dormant for centuries. Characterization of the latter days as the dispensation of the fulness of times hinges in great measure upon the reemergence of the full array of spiritual gifts among mankind which have become anchors in our daily lives of traversing the covenant path in preparation for the Second Coming.

Notes

1. Joseph Smith, as quoted in B. H. Roberts, *A Comprehensive History of the Church*, 1:163.
2. Chauncey C. Riddle, "Prayer," *Ensign*, March 1975; emphasis added.
3. Bruce R. McConkie, *A New Witness for the Articles of Faith* (Salt Lake City: Deseret Book, 1985), 384; emphasis added.
4. Bruce R. McConkie, *Mormon Doctrine*, 2nd ed. (Salt Lake City: Bookcraft, 1966), 315; emphasis added.
5. Hugh Nibley, *Approaching Zion*, vol 9 in *The Collected Works of Hugh Nibley* (Salt Lake City: Deseret Book, 1989), 89–90; emphasis added.
6. Flavius Magnus Aurelius Cassiodorus, *Institutiones,* as quoted in John Bartlett, *Familiar Quotations*, 15th ed. (Boston: Little, Brown and Company, 1980), 130; emphasis added.
7. William J. Conybeare and J. S. Howson, *The Life and Epistles of St. Paul* (Hartford, CT: S. S. Scranton, 1900), 372; emphasis added.
8. John Wesley, as quoted in James E. Talmage, *Articles of Faith, Classics in Mormon Literature* (Salt Lake City: Deseret Book, 1984), 445; emphasis added.

Chapter 11

Covenants and Abrahamic Tests

"Above all else, brethren [and sisters], let us think straight."
*(Last words spoken by Elder Melvin J. Ballard,
grandfather of Acting President of the
Quorum of the Twelve M. Russell Ballard)*[1]

Making covenants is the expression of a *willing* heart; keeping covenants is the expression of a *faithful* heart. One of the ways we might put ourselves at risk is to use only the lap strap of our seatbelt, ignoring the shoulder strap. President M. Russell Ballard reminded us regarding convenient living (lap strap only) versus covenant living (shoulder and lap strap in unison):

> Sometimes we are tempted to let our lives be governed more by convenience than by covenant. It is not always convenient to live gospel standards and stand up for truth and testify of the Restoration. . . . But there is no spiritual power in living by convenience. *The power comes as we keep our covenants.*[2]

Elder Boyd K. Packer stressed the point even more strongly:

> Keep your covenants and you will be safe. Break them and you will not. . . . We are not free to break our covenants and escape the consequences.[3]

Further, alluding to the safety factor of seatbelts, Elder Neal A. Maxwell said, "*Following celestial road signs [covenants] while in telestial traffic jams is not easy."*[4] Another reinforcing comment comes from Elder J. Reuben Clark, who counseled, *"It is covenants, not circumstances that count in this life—and the life beyond."*[5]

As discussed earlier in this book, trusting God is our sure foundation. Making and keeping covenants demonstrates to the Father our commitment to His plan. He will bless us with power to successfully deal with whatever circumstances we encounter in the school of life—lessons that are tailor-made to eventually perfect us in the world to come. Summarizing the words of scholar Scott W. Hahn, Jeffrey M. Bradshaw writes:

> Covenants are not meant merely to bind us to certain behaviors, but, more broadly, to *enable us to establish and maintain eternal relationships of love and service with God and His children.*[6]

As children of our Father in Heaven, we believe in Him, which builds trust in Him. God then offers us an array of covenants to become more like Him. We willingly and of our own accord agreed to abide certain of those covenants during our pre-mortal existence. We "kept our first estate" as we exercised exceeding great faith in Jesus Christ and His voluntary assertion to become our Savior so that we could reenter Father's presence. While here on our earthly home, we agree to abide additional covenants which forge our eternal relationship with God. Such a relationship with God cannot achieve a fulness of His love unless there is unbounded trust. Think for a moment about relationships which are part of your life. Relationships which have endured the vicissitudes of mortality are built with the cement of trust.

Endowed members of the Church today should understand that there is no going back and that there is no neutral ground where one can flee. It would be tantamount to unbuckling the seatbelt. After having been given such great knowledge of the goodness and mysteries (sacred ordinances) of God, we are responsible for keeping our covenants. Drawing on the teachings of Brigham Young, Hugh Nibley warned:

> One who fails to live up to his [or her] covenants tries to hide first by looking for loopholes in the language of the endowment. . . . *There is no way [Brigham Young observes] by which anyone can possibly misunderstand or wrest the language of the*

*covenants, no matter how determined one is to do it. We can ratio-
nalize with great zeal—and that is the next step—but never escape
from our defensive position.*[7]

Elder Ezra Taft Benson warned us that there are apostates within our
midst teaching and expounding apostate doctrines (strange roads leading
away from the covenant path). He continues:

Christ taught that we should be *in* the world but not *of* it. Yet
there are some in our midst who are not so much concerned
about taking the gospel into the world *as they are about bringing
worldliness into the gospel. . . . They want us to be popular [and not
distinct from] with the worldly even though that is impossible, for all
hell would then want to join us.*

Through their own reasoning and a few misapplied scriptures, they try to sell us the precepts and philosophies of men.
They do not feel the Church is progressive enough.[8]

During our premortal state on the day of the great council, we made
covenants with the Almighty because we trusted Him, His plan, and that
He would keep all the promises associated with those covenants. The
Father presented His plan of happiness; we accepted it; it was intended
for every man and woman. We became parties to the salvation process of
every person under that plan. We agreed, right then and there, to not be
only saviors for ourselves but also for the whole human family. The execution of the plan became not merely the Father's work (see Moses 1:39)
and the Savior's work, but also ours by "doing the works of Abraham"
(D&C 132:32).

Abrahamic Covenant

During the ravages and persecution arising in consequence of the exter-
mination order issued by Governor Boggs of Missouri in late 1833, the
Prophet Joseph received Doctrine and Covenants section 101, which
explained why the Saints had not been successful in establishing Zion.
Of particular applicability to our current conversation is the following:

Therefore, they must needs be chastened and tried, even as Abraham, who was commanded to offer up his only son.

For all those who will not endure chastening, but deny me, cannot be sanctified. (D&C 101:4–5; emphasis added)

The Lord is specifically alluding to the Abrahamic covenant established at the time when Abraham "saw that it was needful for me to obtain another place of residence" (Abraham 1:1). That eternal covenant can be summarized as follows:

Land	A strange land . . . I will give unto thy seed after thee for an everlasting possession. (Abraham 2:6)
Posterity	I will make of thee a great nation. (Abraham 2:9)
	Thou shalt be a father of many nations. (Genesis 17:5–6, 16)
	I will multiply thee, and thy seed after thee . . . and if thou canst count the number of sands, so shall be the number of thy seeds. (Abraham 3:14)
	Kings shall come out of thee. (Genesis 17:6)
	Thy seed . . . shall bear this ministry and Priesthood unto all nations. (Abraham 2:9, 11; Genesis 17:7, 16; Abraham 1:4)
	As many as receive this Gospel shall be called after thy name, and shall be accounted thy seed, and shall rise up and bless thee, as their father. (Abraham 2:10; Isaiah 51:1–2)
	He [Abraham] shall command his children . . . and they shall keep the way of the Lord, to do justice and judgement. (Genesis 18:9)
Priesthood and gospel blessings	I will take thee, to put upon thee my name, even the Priesthood. (Abraham 1:18)
	Through thy ministry my name shall be known in the earth forever. (Abraham 1:19)
	I will . . . make thy name great among all nations. (Genesis 12:2)
	I will bless them that bless thee, and curse them that curse thee. (Abraham 2:11; Genesis 12:3)
	This right [of the priesthood] shall continue in thee and in thy seed. (Abraham 2:11)

Salvation and exaltation	In thy seed after thee . . . shall all the families of the earth be blessed." (Abraham 2:11; Genesis 12:3; 18:18; 22:18)
	I will bless thee above measure . . . and in thy seed after thee . . . shall all the families of the earth be blessed, even with the blessings of the Gospel, which are the blessings of salvation, even of life eternal. (Abraham 2:9, 11; Genesis 12:12)
	I am thy shield and thy exceeding great reward. (Genesis 15:1)
	Thy seed shall possess the gate of his enemies. (Genesis 22:17)

What then is the Abrahamic covenant? Elder Bruce R. McConkie explains:

> It is that Abraham and his seed (including those who are adopted [through baptism] into his family) shall have all the blessings of the gospel, of the priesthood, and of eternal life. The gate to eternal life is celestial marriage, which holy order of matrimony enables the family unit to continue in eternity, so that the participating parties may have posterity as numerous as the sands upon the seashore or the stars in heaven.
>
> The Abrahamic covenant enables men and women to create for themselves eternal family units that are patterned after the family of God our Heavenly Father and Mother. A lesser part of the covenant is that the seed of Abraham have the Millennial destiny of inheriting as an everlasting possession the very land of Canaan whereon the feet of the righteous have trod in days gone by.[9]

When we look at the Abrahamic covenant, we can see three groups of applications: individual tests, collective tests (the Church as a whole), and generational (dispensational) tests. Note: "tests" represents the equivalent of demonstrating faith in Jesus Christ and trusting in God, in the components of His plan, and the timing of His plan.

Individual Abrahamic Tests

I have observed, and no doubt you have also, that the prevalence of evidence surrounding individual Abrahamic tests is almost overwhelming:

discerning and then choosing good over evil; making poor choices, which result in consequences such as unhappiness, sickness, loneliness, despair, feelings of hopelessness, unworthiness, and other multitudinous forms of suffering. We see our brothers and sisters struggling with disabilities, deformities, missing limbs, Down syndrome, autism, or cancer, just to name a few. Disappointments in marriage, wayward children, abuse—the list goes on and on. Though from our limited and narrow perspective, these individual tests are often inexplicable and seemingly unjust or inequitable, we must come to know that all are part of the test, and there is more equality in this testing than sometimes we suspect.[10] Our minds and sense of fairness are paralyzed by the thought that these uniquely different tests can somehow be considered equal on the scales of God's justice. Without any doubt, we can be assured that everyone is being tested given their individual circumstances and their unique combination of traits, characteristics, and parameters. Sometimes, when trying to rationalize individual testing, we can also find ourselves erroneously "looking beyond the mark" (Jacob 4:14). In other words, we misunderstand or misinterpret the test. We do not see or understand the individualized tailoring involved. We should remember that the Lord knows us better than we know ourselves.

The Lord explained to Joseph Smith that His people must be "tried" (meaning "purified" according to Webster's 1828 dictionary) in all things (see D&C 136:31). We should remember that *how* individualized testing prepares, tries, or proves us is not always described or explained. It has been my experience that the Lord often provides instructions (commandments) but does not usually give "why" or "how" explanations. A classic example would be why the priesthood was withheld from men of color. And now that all worthy men are privileged to hold the priesthood, we still do not know why that blessing was in abeyance for so long. As the Lord told Moses when he inquired as to how the creation was accomplished: "Here is wisdom and it remaineth in me" (Moses 1:31). End of discussion. Will we be given the reason at some future date? Maybe. But only if it is needful to becoming perfect—that is, complete.

However, we do know that many individual tests can be accounted for when we read about King Hezekiah: "God left him, *to try him that he [Hezekiah] might know what was in his heart*" (2 Chronicles 32:31;

emphasis added). Paul comforts the converts in Thessalonica: "But as we were allowed of God to be put in trust with the gospel . . . not as pleasing men, but God, which *trieth our hearts*" (1 Thessalonians 2:4; emphasis added). Our premortal covenant contains a stipulation that we will totally commit our hearts to God the Father. What should be in our hearts? Trust!

There is a sobering illustration which comes from the life of Oliver Cowdery during the Church council resulting in his excommunication. He said on that sad occasion: "I will not be influenced, governed, or controlled in my *temporal interests* by any ecclesiastical authority or pretended revelation whatever, contrary to my own judgment."[11] Oliver's individual test was to determine whether he would listen to and follow a prophet in all things, not just selective theological ideas. Deciding whether to follow what to him was a temporal not spiritual revelation given to the Prophet Joseph Smith was Oliver's Abrahamic test. He lost understanding and surrendered his heart to Satan.

Collective Abrahamic Tests

With regard to collective Abrahamic tests, presidents of the Church from Brigham Young to Russell M. Nelson have commented regarding a variety of circumstances which have raised their concern about the variety of collective Abrahamic tests that have and will yet challenge the Saints, including but not limited to wealth, peace, the attitude that all is well in Zion, luxury, ease, affluence, etc. Most recently, "the time is coming when those who do not obey the Lord will be separated from those who do" is the warning of President Nelson in reference to the Savior's parable of the wheat and the tares as revealed in Doctrine and Covenants 86:1–7. In the same message in the May 2020 *Ensign*, he said, "Difficult days are ahead. Rarely in the future will it be easy or popular to be a faithful Latter-day Saint [individually or as a people]. [We collectively] will be tested."[12] President Nelson's admonition echoes the counsel of President Gordon B. Hinckley, who prophetically declared:

> I do not believe the time is here when an all-consuming calamity will overtake us. . . .

. . . Peace may be denied for a season. . . . We may even be called on to suffer one way or another [COVID-19 jumps to mind]. . . . *Our safety lies in repentance. Our strength comes of obedience to the commandments of God. . . . This is the crux of the entire matter—obedience to the commandments of God.*[13]

Obedience to God's commandments is nothing more than fulfilling our part of the Abrahamic covenant, the sacred two-way agreement we committed to in the premortal council. The reassuring words of President Lorenzo Snow ring in our ears as he describes keeping our first estate, meaning that we successfully honored our part of the premortal clauses and conditions of the Abrahamic covenant.

We are here because we are worthy to be here, and that arises, to a great extent at least, from the fact that we kept our first estate. *I believe that when you and I were in yonder life we made certain covenants . . . that in this life, when we should be permitted to enter it, we would do what we had done in that life—find out the will of God and conform to it.*[14]

In my mind, I can conceive of how difficult it was to be engaged in the war of words and ideologies that occurred in the premortal world. Yet, we know that we were valiant there and then. Alma taught Zeezrom that we were "prepared from the foundation of the world according to the foreknowledge of God, *on account of their [our] exceeding faith and good works*" (Alma 13:3; emphasis added). So, in these latter days, though society and culture become "unbelievably bad" and "without hope" reminiscent of the era when Mormon and Moroni were the last two faithful Nephites running and hiding to escape the bloodthirsty Lamanites who wanted them dead, we can remain undauntedly faithful and possess vast reservoirs of hope, fueled by lots of chocolate vitamins, to face the coming days with confidence. The question is *not* how bad society and the world will become; rather, the "Abrahamic" interrogatory is "*How good will we as Saints, collectively, be?*" The answer is that we will be valiant again in honoring the promises made connected with the Abrahamic covenant. Why will we be successful, you ask? Because we have been successful before. And we have the chocolate-covered vitamins of the additional covenants we have made here in mortality—baptism and temple endowment to maintain our strength and resolve to keep our covenants.

Generational Abrahamic Tests

Our generational Abrahamic tests include the dangers of assimilation, acceptance, sophistication, and secularization. There is no question that not only is there an abundance of knowledge, but an absolute explosion of information—some true and some not so true, even totally false—associated with the meteoric expansion of the internet. With a perspective more than half a century before its time, author, poet, and dramatist T. S. Eliot insightfully wrote: 'Where is the wisdom we have lost in knowledge? Where is the knowledge we have lost in information?"[15] Will we become pawns addicted to the internet, believing that we can find answers to all our questions by asking Google or Alexa?

Another of our generational tests is the inescapable fact that the Restoration is ongoing. Contrary to the understanding of many, the Restoration was not an event. It did not happen all at once. It was not completed in the days of the prophets Joseph Smith and Brigham Young, nor will it be completed prior to the advent of Jesus Christ at the beginning of the Millennium. President Nelson taught us clearly:

> We're witnesses to a process of restoration. If you think the Church has been fully restored, you're just seeing the beginning. There is much more to come.[16]

We have three roles as part of our generational test associated with the Abrahamic covenant: (1) proclaim the gospel (missionary work), (2) redeem the dead (genealogical and temple work), and (3) perfect the saints (ministering). The test also includes subscribing to and sustaining every "adjustment" to Church policy and procedure that will emanate from the Brethren. Will we recognize the hand of the Lord in continuing to establish and restore His Church as "the stone [that] was cut out of the mountain without [human] hands" (Daniel 2:45) and that will roll forth to fill the whole earth? The wonderful things lying ahead are beyond our current understanding but if we are paying attention, we will recognize the hand of God.

Additional knowledge of any kind throws new light onto what we already know, recontextualizes it, thus helping us understand it differently, and see better where, how, and why things fit together. The burning question is "Will we accept it?" I have come to believe that in most, if not all, situations where the mystery (sacred information) and miracle of having a piece of knowledge relocated from our heads and being "[written] in their hearts" (Jeremiah 31:33), grace is involved. As we do all we can do (see 2 Nephi 25:26 and chapter 5 above), the Lord, in His time, and when we are ready, can and will actually change us, writing on our hearts the knowledge we have carefully stored in our heads. Elder Dallin H. Oaks counseled us: "In all the important decisions in our lives, what is most important is to *do the right thing . . . at the right time.*"[17] It is a marvelous paradox that to ever really know, we must accept that which we yet don't know (see chapter 8 for a discussion of believing before hearing). Sometimes we have trouble figuring out why we must wait; why aren't we allowed to know the answers now? God gives us what we are ready to hear—and no more—because He loves us. Getting more than we are ready to accept or understand either does no good at all—or could potentially cause harm.

Zion = Sacred Land

In the Old Testament, when God established His covenant with Abraham, one of the key elements was the promise of a *sacred land* of inheritance for his posterity. This same component of the promise given to Abraham was renewed with Moses and the children of Israel, which resulted an obsession with the land of Palestine/Israel as being the "place," especially since Jerusalem is where Mount Moriah—the mountain where Abraham sealed his covenant with Yahweh by offering Isaac—is located. What came out of that covenantal view was the temple. Hence, the prayer expressed three times a day by devout Jews includes these words:

Find favor, O Lord our God, in our people Israel and their prayers, and *restore the Temple* service to the innermost chamber of our House [Holy of Holies]. May you accept Israel's burnt offerings and prayer with love and grace; and may the service of your people Israel [in the temple] be ever pleasing to you. May our eyes see your return to Zion. . . . Blessed are you, O Lord, *who restores your presence to Zion.*[18]

In the Book of Mormon, we find this same scenario with Lehi and Nephi, who on more than one occasion when teaching their children refer to having "obtained a land of promise, a land which is choice above all other lands; a land which the Lord God hath covenanted with me should be a land for the inheritance of me seed. Yea, the Lord hath covenanted this land unto me, and to my children forever" (2 Nephi 1:5). And though the Nephi, his family, and other devoted followers are forced to relocate twice, they finally find a safe and peaceful place of residence where immediately begin to build a temple. Why? So they could observe and thereby fulfill the law of Moses, which pointed them to Christ, and having the presence of the Lord to be with them in a "sacred place."

In a conformational pattern, we recall that certain Saints, in the early part of 1831, who comprised the Colesville Branch (New York) were the first group told to gather in Missouri, believing that it would be the promised land, center point of Zion. But, by December 1833, the Saints were being driven out. What we as Saints today learn is that this aspect of the Abrahamic covenant is not about a specific geographic location. God can make any land a land of promise, a holy and sacred land. The geography lesson we are to incorporate is that the covenant's locus (sacred place) is the heart.

There is another dimension of covenants, particularly Abraham's covenant which deserves mention in this discussion. One of Abraham's blessings is that all his progeny would be blessed with the gospel and the priesthood. It stands to reason that the optimal manner wherein this blessing could be realized would be for his descendants to be living together in the land (Canaan) he was promised. What happened instead? The children of Abraham, including the house of Israel, have been dispersed across the face of the earth, among all nations and islands of the sea. This scattering became a pattern of movement necessary for the fulfillment of the Father's covenant. Without the Diaspora (more broadly conceived than just the ten tribes of Israel), there would be no way to actuate the promise made to Abraham that through his seed all nations of the earth would be blessed. This purpose for the Abrahamic covenant is found three times in the Book of Mormon; and in each case, it is associated with the necessity of scattering Abraham's seed so that all can hear and decide whether or not they will exercise their free choice to accept the gospel of Christ.

How else can the phenomenon that 60 percent of temples are now outside the United States be explained? Abraham's seed are found in virtually every country in the world; and when missionaries are able to enter those nations and preach the gospel of the restoration, there are people with "believing blood" (Abraham's seed) who respond to the message and join the Church. They are "grabbing hold" of the iron rod and beginning to walk on the covenant path toward the tree of life. Their incomplete knowledge and understanding of the Abrahamic covenant gained from studying the Bible or other books prepared by the Lord is enhanced and enlarged by the restoration of "plain and precious things" found in the Book of Mormon. Thus, we can see that the scattering is how Abraham's seed is blessing the nations; and the gathering is being accomplished country by country as temples are built in foreign lands opening up the privileges and ordinances to "seal" families together, which is the whole point of the continuing Restoration of the gospel—to prepare the entire earth for the Second Coming of Christ.

Notes

1. Melvin J. Ballard, as quoted in M. Russell Ballard, "Let Us Think Straight" (Brigham Young University devotional, August 20, 2013), speeches.byu.edu.
2. M. Russell Ballard, "Like a Flame Unquenchable," *Ensign*, May 1999; emphasis added.
3. Boyd K. Packer, "Covenants," *Ensign*, November 1990.
4. Neal A. Maxwell, "Not Withstanding My Weakness," *Ensign*, November 1976; emphasis added.
5. J. Reuben Clark, "To Them of the Last Wagon," in Conference Report, October 1947; emphasis added.
6. Jeffrey M. Bradshaw, "If 'All Are Alike Unto God,' Why Were Special Promises Reserved for Abraham's Seed?" *Meridian Magazine*, February 11, 2018, ldsmag. com; emphasis added.
7. Hugh W. Nibley, "On the Sacred and the Symbolic," in *Temples of the Ancient World: Ritual and Symbolism*, ed. Donald W. Parry (Salt Lake City: Deseret Book, 1994), 610; emphasis added.

8. Ezra Taft Benson, in Conference Report, April 1969; emphasis added.

9. Bruce R. McConkie, *A New Witness for the Articles of Faith* (Salt Lake City: Deseret Book, 1985), 505; emphasis added.

10. See Boyd K. Packer, "The Choice," *Ensign*, November 1980.

11. Oliver Cowdery to Edward Partridge, Far West, Missouri, April 12, 1838, josephsmithpapers.org; emphasis added.

12. Russell M. Nelson, "The Future of the Church: Preparing the World for the Savior's Second Coming," *Ensign*, April 2020.

13. Gordon B. Hinckley, "The Times in Which We Live," *Ensign*, January 2002; emphasis added.

14. Lorenzo Snow, in *Collected Discourses Delivered by President Wilford Woodruff, His Two Counselors, the Twelve Apostles, and Others*, comp. and ed. Brian H. Stuy, 5 vols. (Burbank, CA: B. H. S. Publishing, 1988), 4:55; emphasis added.

15. T. S. Eliot, *The Rock* (London: Faber & Faber, 1934).

16. Russell M. Nelson, in "Latter-day Saint Prophet, Wife and Apostle Share Insights of Global Ministry," October 30, 2018, www.Newsroom.ChurchofJesusChrist.org.

17. Dallin H. Oaks, "Timing" (Brigham Young University devotional, January 29, 2002), speeches.byu.edu; emphasis added.

18. Jon Levinson, *Sinai and Zion: An Entry into the Jewish Bible* (San Francisco: HarperSanFrancisco, 1985), 179; emphasis added.

Chapter 12
Commandments and Service

Let us be reassured that the everyday keeping of the commandments and the doing of
our duties [service] is what it is all about.

(Neal A. Maxwell)[1]

We know that keeping the commandments demonstrates faith in Jesus Christ. Service is a primary means of keeping the commandments (e.g., being a loving neighbor). Thus, commandments are ultimately about service to others. They are two sides of the same coin. Vitamins are a valuable navigational tool to assist us in this divine process.

Book of Commandments

Just nineteen months after the Church was organized, a special conference of the elders was held in Hiram, Ohio, on November 1, 1831. The purpose was to determine the Lord's will about publishing the sixty-five revelations which had been received since the initial events had inaugurated the Restoration. Their effort was to become the Book of Commandments, the predecessor of today's Doctrine and Covenants. As in all circumstances when we study the scriptures, we must put them into context. First, we recall that the triggering situation for Doctrine and Covenants section 1 (known as the Preface) was that several of the Brethren in attendance at the Hiram Conference attempted to write a preface for the Book of Commandments. However, their efforts proved to be futile. During the conference, the Lord dictated through Joseph

Smith the words of Section 1: the Preface to the Book of Commandments and the Doctrine and Covenants.

Second, we must remember that all Church members at this time (1831) were converts from other faith traditions. In those religious organizations, members were accustomed to twelve commandments—namely, the Decalogue (see Exodus 20), love God (Deuteronomy 6:5), and love thy neighbor (Leviticus 19:18). Now, as newly baptized converts, they were facing a flood of new commandments, and they felt completely overwhelmed, to say the least. Thus, in section 1, the Lord, departing from His norm, which is to not supply explanations as to the reasons for commandments, tells his young prophet and his followers why commandments are given. We begin with verse 17 (emphasis added):

Wherefore, I the Lord, knowing the calamity which should come upon the inhabitants of the earth, called upon my servant Joseph Smith, Jun., and spake unto him from heaven, and *gave unto him commandments*;

And also gave commandments to others [through Joseph], that they should proclaim these things unto the world . . .

. . . Man should . . . neither trust in the arm of flesh . . .

But that every man might speak in the name of God . . .

That faith also might increase in the earth;

That mine everlasting covenant might be established;

That the fulness of my gospel might be proclaimed . . . unto the ends of the world . . .

. . . *These commandments are of me, and were given to my servants* . . .

And inasmuch as they erred it might be made known;

And inasmuch as they sought wisdom they might be instructed;

And inasmuch as they sinned they might be chastened, that they might repent;

And inasmuch as they were humble they might be made strong, and blessed from on high, and receive knowledge from time to time.

And what does this look like? The Lord's answer is in verse 37: *"Search these commandments, for they are true and faithful, and the prophecies and promises which are in them shall all be fulfilled."* The Lord directly promised the Saints that humble and prayerful inquiries about the revelations would result in answers and explanations to understand three things: (1) if they erred, (2) if they sought wisdom, and (3) if they sinned they would be chastened. Such is the curriculum of becoming like God. Eat more vitamins!

Sacred Numbers

With the foregoing as a background, let us now consider the Book of Mormon. It was interesting to me that during the course of my 2020 *Come Follow Me* rereading of the introductory chapters of 1 Nephi—which most of us can probably quote since we have read them so many times in our repeated resolutions and multiple efforts to study the Book of Mormon—how many specific commandments the Lord gave to Lehi to "lead him by HIS hand" during the eight-year journey to finally arrive in the promised land. Allow me to summarize:

- Commanded to go on a mission of indeterminate length and preach repentance to the inhabitants of the city of Jerusalem
- Commanded to pack up his family and leave Jerusalem
- Commanded to leave most of his gold and other precious things behind
- Commanded which direction to initially travel
- Commanded to send his three sons back to Jerusalem to obtain the plates of brass
- Commanded to send his three sons back to invite Ishmael's family to join them in the wilderness
- Commanded when to leave the valley of Lemuel
- Through the operation of the Liahona, commanded the two families about which direction to travel on their way to the seacoast
- Commanded when and how to build the ship, not after the manner of men
- Commanded when to board the ship, and then something very interesting

- "After we had prepared all things, much fruits and meat from the wilderness, and honey in abundance; and *provisions according to that which the Lord had commanded*" (1 Nephi 18:6; emphasis added)
- Commanded that plates be made, and a history of Lehi be compiled as soon as they arrived

Lehi was given twelve commandments. In ancient Hebrew, Israelite, and Jewish culture, the number twelve is sacred, just as the numbers three, seven, and forty are. Twelve denotes and represents God, Heaven, perfection, entirety, authority, and cosmic government. Therefore, it is not coincidental nor accidental that our calendar has twelve months; there are twelve commandments—the Decalogue plus "love god" and "love your neighbor"; there are twelve tribes; Jesus had twelve Apostles; and baptismal fonts in temples rest on the backs of twelve oxen. You get the message. Thus, having twelve of something was significant to Lehi and Nephi.

It is amazing how specific the Lord was in accomplishing the objective of preserving a branch of the tree by planting it in another part of His vineyard. Truly, the Lord was leading them by His hand—and He will do the same for each of us in our journey to go back home. It struck me how many times the Lord gave specific directions to Lehi—particularly the commandment associated with getting on the ship. He even told them specifically which provisions to load and take with them (see 1 Nephi 18:6).

Now, I realize that Lehi's circumstance is not a common everyday situation; it was necessary for the Lord to outline step-by-step what was to be done along with specific timing of when those commandments were to be implemented in order to achieve the objectives of Lehi's mission. Consequently, we should acknowledge that the Lord can and probably will be just as specific with us, as needed, when helping us to "Hear Him" and doing what He asks of us.

I also noticed that there are eighty-four verses in 1 Nephi 2–4, which describe Lehi preaching in and then having to leave Jerusalem, sending his sons back to get the brass plates from Laban, and sending his sons back a second time to invite the family of Ishmael to leave and join Lehi in the wilderness. In those eighty-four verses, the word *commandment* (and related constructs) is used twenty-one times—a usage factor of 25 percent. It occurred to me that here was a message which I had overlooked. To explain requires that I set the stage.

Nephi Keeps the Lord's Commandment

The third commandment given by the Lord to Lehi, following the commandment to preach repentance to the inhabitants of Jerusalem, and then the commandment to pack up his family and leave, was the commandment to obtain the brass plates. So Laman, Lemuel, and Nephi (recall that three witnesses are necessary to establish the veracity of assertions under the law of Moses, see Deuteronomy 17:6) are given a priesthood assignment by their father, Lehi, to return to the Holy City and retrieve the brass plates from Laban, the custodian and caretaker of the brass plates. In response to that sacred assignment, Lehi's three sons journeyed for three days back to Jerusalem and arranged an audience with Laban. As emissaries of the prophet Lehi, they delivered the commandment received by their father. Now, there can be no doubt that Laban knew who these three young men were, and he knew who Lehi was. So why did Lehi send three of his sons? I doubt that the brass plates were of such enormous weight that it would take three strapping young men to carry them. The reason for three of them was to comply with the requirement to have three witnesses according to the law of Moses to testify of the Lord's revelation and confirm to Laban that he should relinquish the brass plates. Laban initially rejected Laman's message from Lehi for a variety of reasons, including that only Laman (not all three brothers) presented the request. It should be noted that later when the threesome returned with their wealth, Laban again rejected the Lord's will being specifically communicated to him, which was tantamount to denying one of God's prophets.

After Laban refused the initial request to surrender the brass plates as the Lord had commanded through Lehi the prophet, the three sons go to their land of inheritance and gather up the family's gold, silver, and other precious things left behind hoping to effect an exchange with Laban, which we know did not achieve the commanded objective. Laban succumbed to Satan's temptation—namely, to "get gain"** for when he saw that Lehi's wealth was "exceedingly great, . . . he did lust after it" (1 Nephi 3:25). Strike three! Laban sinned twice by failing to comply with a direct commandment of God delivered by priesthood messengers of a prophet of God and then by "seeking gain," which culminated in robbery of Lehi's wealth, which was a capital offense punishable by death under the law of Moses. The consequence was being transferred to the spirit world by Nephi who humbly kept the commandment—obtain the plates.

There have been innumerable pages written discussing the question of "Why kill Laban?", addressing everything from moral issues associated with taking someone's life, to the ethical views of that behavior, to the legality of such a precipitous action, and to speculate as to the existence of other ways that the plates may have been obtained that did not involve executing Laban. But all that discussion aside, the bottom line was this: would Nephi and his brothers obey the commandment of God, regardless of whether they were given a "heads-up" that their assignment would eventually involve slaying Laban? The Spirit did "constrain" (1 Nephi 4:10) Nephi to perform the execution with the explanation given in verse 13. Instead of stopping at the end of verse 13, the reader should continue with verse 14, which contains the key (a suggestion when reading scripture is to always read several verses prior to and subsequent to the verse which seems to be the Lord's explanation):

> And now, when I, Nephi, had heard these words [verse 13], I remembered [oops, there is that pesky word—*remember*] the words of the Lord which he spake unto me in the wilderness, saying that: *Inasmuch as thy seed shall keep my commandments, they shall prosper.* (1 Nephi 4:14; emphasis added)

And this principle is further ratified in verse 17: "that I might obtain the records *according to His commandment.*" Nephi's actions were driven

---

** It is intriguing that the third event translated by Joseph Smith—after Lehi's missionary assignment to call Jerusalem to repentance, and then to leave the land of their inheritance—was the narrative of obtaining the brass plates and how one man wanted them for their monetary wealth and used force to obtain wealth in contravention to what he knew was wrong as the custodian of those prophetic writings and genealogies.

solely by his motivation to keep God's commandments, whether he could rationalize them or not as being moral, ethical, etc., or engage in a fruitless mind game to develop a strategy other than killing Laban to obtain the plates. A tremendous lesson for us—right out of the starting gate, as it were.

There was another insight that jumped out to me as I continued to study 1 Nephi. After being so specific in what to do, when to do it, and what to take with them, it was interesting that when Nephi was given the commandment to build a ship, he inquired of the Lord as to where he should go to find ore to make tools (see 1 Nephi 17:9). However, Elder L. Tom Perry noted something interesting related to making tools:

> I have sometimes wondered what *would have happened if Nephi had asked the Lord for tools instead of a place where to find ore to make the tools.* I doubt the Lord would have honored Nephi's request. You see, the Lord knew that Nephi could make the [necessary] tools, and it is seldom the Lord will do something for us that we can do for ourselves.[2]

The Lord often expects us to "make the tools" because we have the appropriate vitamins already available to us.

"To Serve You Is Perfect Freedom"

One of the prayers in the Church of England liturgy opens with this powerful phrase: "To know you is eternal life and to serve you is perfect freedom."[3] Every disciple chooses to serve through acts of free will, which are not compromised by any degrading effects of servility. Christians are called upon to be faithful, and obedience becomes paramount. Service to others will surely bring us closer to God especially when motivated by an unselfish sense of personal compassion.

> The ultimate purpose of the gospel of Jesus Christ is to cause the sons and daughters of God to become as Christ is. Those who see religious purpose only in terms of ethical service as the basis for the relationship between man and fellowman may miss that divinely ordained possibility.[4]

Recall that the second commandment is to love [serve] our neighbor. As Bruce C. Hafen wrote:

It is quite possible to render charitable—even "Christian"— service without developing deeply ingrained and permanent Christlike character. Paul understood this when he warned against giving all one's goods to feed the poor without true charity. . . . We can give without loving, but we cannot love without giving. . . . We then act charitably toward others, not merely because we think we should, but because that is the way we are.[5]

The Prophet Joseph taught:

If any person will build up others; benefit, bless, and permanently aggrandize others he [she] will be aggrandized eternally, and that is the only principle . . . upon which it can be done and remain forever.[6]

Christlike service sanctifies both the giver and the receiver. Those who involve themselves in the work of the Master receive the approbation of the Master. President David O. McKay once observed: "If you want to love God, you have to learn to love and serve the people. That is the way you show your love for God."[7] Our service is centered in Christ, our eye single to His glory. Deeds of service, works of faith, and acts of kindness toward others are so much more effective and pure when grounded in the love of Deity. Service (ministering) is absolutely essential if we desire to follow our Lord and Master. But that service is lasting and life-changing only when it is motivated by pure love.

One last note: service is a two-sided coin, as mentioned above. One side, perhaps the side we assign more importance to, is of course the *giving* of service to others in need, whether it be physical, emotional, or social. But the other side of the coin, which I fear is often not emphasized sufficiently, is the *receiving* of service from others. Learning to be grateful and humble as a recipient of service is just as vital and essential to Christlike service as is being a giver.

The heading of this section—"To serve you is perfect freedom"—begs the question, "What is perfect freedom?" Perhaps one important answer is the "freedom to become." Freedom to become is what we inherently have within ourselves to become. We are grateful for many things that we have freedom "from." However, in the journey of mortality, freedom to *become* matters more than freedom *from*. The link between God's comfort to us and our rendering comfort or service to others is a powerful idea. Such encouragement to magnify God's love through us to other people comes in this marvelous counsel found in Dostoyevsky's *The Brothers Karamazov*. Father Zossima is speaking to a woman who fears greatly because of her perceived inadequacies, and thus finds herself cut off, distant, and seemingly unable to successfully reach out to other people:

> Fear nothing and never be afraid; and don't fret. . . . Can there be a sin which could exceed the love of God? Think only of repentance . . . dismiss fear altogether. Believe that God loves you as you cannot conceive . . . what has been said of old that over one repentant sinner there is more joy in heaven than over ten righteous men. Go, and fear not. Be not bitter against men. Be not angry if you are wronged. Forgive . . .
>
> If you are penitent, you love. And if you love you are of God. All things are atoned for, all things are saved by love. If I, a sinner, even as you are, am tender with you and have pity on you, how much more will God. *Love is such a priceless treasure that you can redeem the whole world by it, and expatiate not only your own sins but the sins of others. . . . Go, and be not afraid.*[8]

Confidence is a gift from God to enable us to serve others. Dostoyevsky reinforces this important principle, not only for believers like you and me, but with the unbelieving woman who has lost her faith and wants to know how to regain it. Not surprisingly, Father Zossima counsels her to serve, to seek out, to comfort others with the very comfort she herself desires to have.

> *By the experience of active love. Strive to love your neighbour actively and indefatigably.* In as far as you advance in love you will grow surer of the reality of God and of the immortality of your soul. If you attain to perfect self-forgetfulness in the love of your neighbour, then you will believe without doubt, and no doubt can enter your soul. This has been tried. This is certain.[9]

Such is the blessing of the freedom to *become*, not just to have the freedom *from* the cares of the world, physical limitations, emotional struggles, economic setbacks, dysfunctional families, etc. Elder Holland related a story shared with him by a BYU student during his tenure as president of the University:

> Two young women students understood that God's comfort and compassion often needs to come to others through us. These two young ladies were the sort of Christians we all could and should emulate. They even studied the scriptures every day for the express purpose of learning more of the attributes and doctrines of Jesus Christ. Quietly, but inevitably, those divine attributes rub off. The two students, of course, had their share of difficulties, some of which were not small, but not so serious, perhaps, as the struggles of someone else.
>
> As they walked around the Provo Temple one evening, they saw a young American Indian girl, a freshman at BYU, who was sitting outside the gates of the temple, bathing the grass with her tears. She was an excellent student, and all her life she had dreamed of attending BYU. Finally, her dream had become a reality. But now, mere weeks into the semester, she had received terrible grades on her midterms; and far away, her family was falling apart, with her mother in danger for her life at the hands of her drunken father. The girl's money was gone, employment was nowhere to be found, she had no friends, and now, to top things off, her health and her grades were suffering because of all these external pressures. No wonder she wept! No wonder she had gone to the temple grounds to pray.
>
> The two young ladies, bearing in their countenances the images of comforting angels, stopped to talk. The conversation went on for more than an hour; then the three went their separate ways. However, every few days, whether they had time or not, the two young women would visit this fearful and distraught Indian girl or leave her a note on the door to her apartment. Each time the message was essentially the same, though not precisely in these words: "We love you. God loves you. Let your heart be

comforted, 'for all flesh is in mine hands.' (D&C 101:16) "God is our refuge and strength, a very present help in trouble . . . be still and know that I am God" (Psalm 46:1 & 10).

Of course, trials did not disappear overnight; some of them did not ever improve. But this young Indian student changed. I do not know what she knew of God before that lonely night in October—obviously, she knew enough to pray—but she discovered something about Heavenly Father that she did not know before. In the form of two young women just her age she saw "the God of all comfort." Implanted deep in her soul is the assurance that He sent those two disciples to her rescue, two young students whose last names she does not even know. And she knows that God sent them because He loves her.[10]

This incident causes us to recall the words of Abraham Lincoln in his first inaugural address:

We are not enemies, but friends. We must not be enemies. Though passion may have strained it must not break our bonds of affection. *The mystic chords of memory . . . will yet swell . . . when again touched, as surely they will be, by the better angels of our nature.*[11]

As members of The Church of Jesus Christ of Latter-day Saints, it is impossible to miss hearing the message of service which is proclaimed by inspired prophets, seers, and revelators. It is repeated more than once or twice in general conference sermons. Ward and stake councils have service opportunities as a fixed item of discussion on the agenda of every meeting. Missionaries now do more than just proselyte. They are rendering service in a variety of ways. We are even serving those who have gone before through the technology of FamilySearch. How marvelous the gospel in that it reveals the interconnectedness of commandments and service!

Notes

1. Neal A. Maxwell, *Notwithstanding My Weakness* (Salt Lake City: Deseret Book, 1981), 18.

2. L. Tom Perry, "Becoming Self-Reliant," *Ensign*, November 1991; emphasis added.

3. *The Alternative Service Book 1980* (Cambridge: Cambridge University Press, 1980), 59.

4. Robert L. Millet, "This Is My Gospel," in *The Book of Mormon: 3 Nephi 9–30, This Is My Gospel* (Provo, UT: Religious Studies Center, 1993), 1–24.

5. Bruce C. Hafen, *The Broken Heart: Applying the Atonement to Life's Experiences* (Salt Lake City: Deseret Book, 1989), 196–97.

6. Diary of O. B. Huntington, unpublished typescript, 2 vols (Provo, UT: Brigham Young University, 1942), 2:212, as quoted in Truman G. Madsen, "The Suffering Servant" in *The Redeemer—Reflections on the Life and Teachings of Jesus the Christ* (Salt Lake City: Deseret Book, 2000), 231.

7. As quoted by President Harold B. Lee, in Conference Report, April 1973, 180.

8. Fyodor Dostoyevsky, *The Brothers Karamazov*, trans. Constance Garnett (New York: The Macmillan Company, 1922), 48; emphasis added.

9. Dostoyevsky, 53; emphasis added.

10. Adapted from Jeffrey R. Holland and Patricia T. Holland, *On Earth as It Is in Heaven* (Salt Lake City: Deseret Book, 1989), 44–47.

11. Abraham Lincoln, "First Inaugural Address of Abraham Lincoln," March 4, 1861, avalon.law.yale.edu/19th_century/lincoln1.asp.

Chapter 13

"Hope"

Hope is hearing the music of the future;
faith is dancing to it today.

(Bishop Bill Frey)[1]

Hope is frequently mentioned in the scriptures as the middle component of the Pauline triad of virtues: faith, hope, and charity. However, it does not seem to get a fair share of the headlines and column space in gospel discussions. We know that hope not only brings comfort, peace, and assurance, but it is also essential to salvation. Moroni taught, "Wherefore man [or woman] must *hope*, or he [or she] cannot receive an inheritance in the place thou hast prepared" (Ether 12:32). C. S. Lewis ratifies this point:

> *Hope is one of the Theological virtues.* This means that a continual looking forward to the eternal world is not (as some modern people think) a form of escapism or wishful thinking, but one of the things a Christian is meant to do.[2]

To lay additional framework for our discussion of hope, let us review the words of Elder Neal A. Maxwell:

> It is well, therefore, to ponder the status of hope in our present human context God's commandments seem unimportant to many. . . .
>
> Real hope keeps us "anxiously engaged" in good causes even when these appear to be losing causes on the mortal scoreboard (see D&C 58:27). Likewise, real hope is much more than

wishful musing. It stiffens, not slackens, the spiritual spine. Hope is serene, not giddy, eager without being naïve, and pleasantly steady without being smug. Hope is realistic anticipation which takes the form of determination—not only to survive adversity but, moreover, to "endure . . . well" to the end (D&C 121:8). . . .

Real hope inspires quiet Christian service, not flashy public fanaticism. Finley Peter Dunne impishly observed, "A fanatic is a man who does what he thinks the Lord would do if He knew the facts." . . .

Indeed, when we are unduly impatient [lacking or waning in hope] with an omniscient God's timing, we really are suggesting that we know what is best. Strange isn't it—we who wear wristwatches seek to counsel Him who oversees cosmic clocks and calendars. . . .

The truly hopeful . . . work amid surrounding decay at having strong and happy families. . . .

We may not be able to fix the whole world, but we can strive [and hope] to fix what may be amiss in our own families. Tolkien reminds us: "It is not our part to master all the tides of the world, but to do what is in us for the succor of those years wherein we are set, uprooting the evil in the fields that we know, so that those who live after may have clean earth to till. What weather they shall have is not ours to rule." . . .

Whatever our particular furrow, we can, in Paul's words, "plow in hope," not looking back, and refusing to let yesterday hold tomorrow hostage (1 Cor. 9:10).[3]

To me hope is faith in action. It takes faith to another level. It is a more potent vitamin.

Discerning between Good and Evil

One of the "hopes" we all share is to be able to judge between good and evil. Judgment is given to every individual. We all have the means to judge between good and evil without having to rely on some outside resource. Mormon in his discourse to his son Moroni in chapter 7 of the book of

Moroni identifies "the way" to judge. In verse 15, he offers encouragement and hope to his son by telling him that the way to judge is simple and readily understood: "It is given unto you to judge, that ye may know good from evil; and *the way to judge is as plain*, that ye may know with a perfect knowledge, as the daylight is from the dark night" (Moroni 7:15; emphasis added). Furthermore, "the way" to judge, if properly applied, results in perfect knowledge. Hence, we, like Moroni, do not need to be concerned about whether we will end up with just a good guess as to what is good or evil; rather, we will know the difference without a doubt. That perfect knowledge results in a clear distinction between what is good and what is evil. Mormon then indicates in verse 16 that "the way" to judge is to assess if (1) it invites to do good and (2) persuades to believe in Christ. On the surface, this can appear to be circular reasoning. However, on a deeper level, Mormon is referring to two "difference judgments" associated with discerning good from evil:

1. Distinguishing between the NATURE of good and evil
2. Identifying the SOURCE of good and evil

As to step 1 of "the way"—we all have available to us the Gift of the Holy Ghost and the Spirit of God. Accordingly, we can search diligently using the Light of Christ and the brightness of the Holy Ghost's illumination to ascertain the "nature" of something as being either good or evil (see verses 16, 18, and 19).

Regarding step 2 of "the way," verse 14 becomes illuminating: "Take heed . . . that ye do not judge that which is evil to be of God, or that which is good and of God to be of the devil." Mormon is warning his son (and us) that if we only discern the nature of good from evil and not recognize its "source," we run the risk of thinking that "the devil might be deceiving me to do something good for some evil purpose of his," or rationalizing that "I know this is an evil thing to do, but perhaps it is the Lord's will that I do it." We should recognize that the "source" of good and evil is a critical piece of knowledge which can be gained as we become more proficient in the process of receiving personal revelation. A truly valuable vitamin.

Faith Precedes Hope

In Moroni 7:40–42, Mormon teaches his son Moroni about hope. He emphasizes that hope does not precede faith; otherwise, he would have discussed hope before faith. Verse 42 unmistakably states that "without faith there cannot be any hope." The object of *hope* is to be lifted up by the power of the atoning blood of Jesus Christ to eternal life, which is based on the foundation of faith in the Savior of the world. Hope is the natural consequence of having faith in Jesus Christ and His Atonement. We are not to sojourn here in mortality constantly doubting whether we are good enough to return to Heavenly Father's presence and share eternal life with Him. We are to develop *hope* that we will be raised to eternal life, not because we are so good that we have qualified for (the Mormon checklist of things to do before we die) or earned it through our own efforts. With faith as our foundation, we develop *hope* that Jesus's crucifixion and resurrection planted the tree of life at the end of the covenant path where we will eventually partake of the most desirable fruit.

It is by virtue of *hope* that we avail ourselves of the two blessings that are appended to and flow from Christ's atoning sacrifice. The first blessing is unconditional: rising from the dead to live in immortal bodies. This gift is given freely to everyone who has been and will yet be born on the earth. It is extended to all by virtue of mercy which is the source of all our blessings. The second blessing is conditional. It requires (a) our participation; (b) being strengthened and becoming sanctified; and (c) choosing to invite and then permit the Lord's grace to perfect us.

First let us consider "participation." This condition relates to our repenting and reconciling ourselves to God. Our repentance is matched by God's willingness to forgive based on the merits of Jesus Christ. Our repentance does not repay Christ for His suffering for our sins and transgression; neither does it mean that we are "earning" His grace.

Second, being strengthened and becoming sanctified. This is an ongoing process, not an event—unfortunately, this is a frequently misunderstood element of Christ's Atonement. The process is enabled and becomes efficacious through a relationship with Christ based on making and keeping covenants. Partaking of the sacrament is our weekly opportunity to renew and refresh our part of the covenant of baptism—namely, "willing to take upon us His name."

Perhaps, I can throw a little brighter light on this subject. Note that it says be *willing to take* upon us His name. "Willing to take" implies something yet to happen; it is future tense. Where does the actual "taking upon us His name" happen? Answer = In the temple when we participate in making covenants while receiving our endowment. We refresh that willingness each time we go to the temple and act as a proxy for someone beyond the veil of death. We also promise to always remember Him and keep His commandments (discussed in chapter 11). God then promises that we will always have His Spirit to be with us to continually nourish us and enable our ability to know how to identify the source of good and evil.

Hope Lifts Us Up and Gives Us Courage

We find ourselves being strengthened by the Lord in our afflictions (see Exodus 4:2–7 and 19:4–6; Mosiah 24:13; and Isaiah 41:10). The Lord also delivers us from bondage. President Dieter F. Uchtdorf explained,

> Hope is not knowledge, but rather the abiding trust that the Lord will fulfill His promise to us. . . . It is believing and expecting that our prayers will be answered. It is manifest in confidence, optimism, enthusiasm, and patient perseverance.[4]

It is this type of *hope* that fortifies Saints to live the gospel, be productive, and illuminate a despondent world by being "lifted up" (Moroni 9:25) by Christ. This type of hope is necessary given the varying circumstances which life imposes upon all of us. This hope is indispensable for parents yearning for a wayward son or daughter to come home, or a mother who calls the hospital only to find her child is on an organ transplant waiting list of several hundred, or a father who is trying to focus on the special, rather than all the needs, when caring for a child with special needs. To be lifted up is not to be rescued from burdens, but rather to be encouraged and motivated within them. The qualities of optimism, enthusiasm, and perseverance converging and centered in the atoning sacrifice of Christ allows individuals to find true and lasting hope. President Monson teaches that having a hope in Christ and a testimony centered in him provides the guidance and supplies the courage to "be faithful in Christ" and to have the assurance that "Christ [will] lift thee up" (Moroni 9:25). After giving several examples of scriptural Saints who remained righteous in difficult circumstances, President Thomas S. Monson explains:

> Perhaps each of these accounts is crowned by the example of Moroni, who had the courage to persevere to the end in righteousness (See Moro. 1–10).
>
> All were fortified by the words of Moses: "Be strong and of a good courage, fear not, nor be afraid . . . : for the Lord thy God, he it is that doth go with thee; he will not fail thee, nor forsake thee" (Deut. 31:6). He did not fail them. He will not fail us. He did not forsake them. He will not forsake us. . . .
>
> It is this sweet assurance [hope] that can guide you and me—in our time, in our day, in our lives. Of course we will face fear, experience ridicule, and meet opposition. Let us have the courage to defy the consensus, the courage to stand for principle. Courage, not compromise, brings the smile of God's approval. Courage becomes a living and an attractive virtue when it is regarded not only as a willingness to die manfully, but also as a determination to live decently. A moral coward is one who is afraid to do what he thinks is right because others will disapprove or laugh. Remember that all men have their fears, but those who face their fears with dignity have courage as well.[5]

Hope centered in Christ provided the necessary courage for Moroni to remain faithful though alone for at least twenty years after his father died. The same hope and courage must grow and flourish in individuals who experience grief and sorrow in the latter days. We learn that despondency, dejection, depression, and a life void of faith does not produce the hope necessary to overcome. Living the gospel requires courage and effort in eras of wickedness; however, such wickedness cannot quench hope placed in the Savior. Mormon's message rings true: may the "hope of his glory and of eternal life, rest in your mind forever" (Moroni 9:25). Ultimately, we have hope in Christ's Atonement because our faith is unfalteringly anchored in believing that the Crucifixion and Resurrection of Jesus Christ actually happened.

We Are the Hope

We are all familiar with the incident involving the Apostle Thomas, who was not present in the upper room the first time that the resurrected Christ appeared to His apostles to provide them sure and undeniable evidence of His Resurrection. When told by some of his colleagues that they had seen and touched the resurrected Jesus, Thomas exhibited his lack of hope with his statement, "Except I shall see in his hands the print of the nails, and put my finger into the print of the nails, and thrust my hand into his side, I will not believe" (John 20:25)—meaning he wanted concrete evidence. A loving Jesus did not deny Thomas what he asked for. You want evidence, Thomas? Very well, here it is. Here are the wounds in my hands, feet, and side that love has borne; here are the marks of what it cost to complete my mission of redemption. He gave Thomas what he needed: evidence of a living Jesus, a loving Jesus, a Jesus who had done everything that the Father wanted to be done as a part of the plan.

The question for us, as we assimilate a deeper measure of hope in our lives is, "How can we be the kind of evidence of Christ's gospel to the world after the manner of evidence that Jesus was for Thomas"? Will we show to the world evidence that Christ really rose from the dead and lives today? Can we show the signs of His love? Will we reach our hands in compassion and service? Will we invite those whose hearts have grown shrunken and shriveled with sorrow and disbelief to come and see what Jesus's ultimate atoning sacrifice has done and continues to do? In short, will our lives be evidence of the "Hope of Israel?" (*Hymns*, no. 259).

In chapter 1 of this book, I mentioned several pieces of knowledge that were revealed to me as I prepared and presented a series of discussions on the First Vision for my gospel doctrine study group. However, I did not include one particular morsel in that list because I wanted to elaborate on it here. It involves something that Joseph Smith did not specifically ask for. Just like He did for Thomas, Jesus gave Joseph evidence of His Resurrection. I believe that it would have been impossible for Joseph not to have seen the marks in Jesus's hands and feet. There is no doubt that

Joseph believed and had faith in Jesus Christ, which provided the basis for his hope of the reality of His Resurrection. But now he was given solid evidence for that hope and could testify to the world that Jesus lives! That He was resurrected and now has a glorious, eternal, and celestial body! Thus, hope for Latter-day Saints is not wishful thinking or mere blind optimism. It is a mode of knowing—knowing that all things are possible. Hope has earned its place in the faith-hope-charity triad.

"I Cannot Come Down"

The prophet Nehemiah of the Old Testament provides a wonderful example of maintaining an attitude of hope, which sustained his commitment to and kept him focused on an important task needing to be accomplished for the benefit of the children of Israel.

> Though the temple had been rebuilt and dedicated in Jerusalem by exiles who had returned from Babylon seventy years earlier under the benevolent decrees of Kings Cyrus and Darius, the city walls had never been rebuilt. This failure to rebuild those walls was due primarily to the antagonism and interference of some of the inhabitants of areas around Jerusalem. Those most difficult to deal with were the Jews who settled in Samaria after the Assyrians had taken the Northern Kingdom into captivity (approx. 600 BC). In 445 BC, during the reign of King Artaxerxes in the Persian Empire, a Jew named Nehemiah held the high office of cupbearer to the king at the palace of Shushan. Some men came to the palace and told Nehemiah the sorry state of Jews who had returned from captivity. "The remnant that returned is in great affliction and reproach," they described to Nehemiah. "The walls of Jerusalem are broken down and the city gates have been burned." Nehemiah wept for the hardships of his people fasting and praying for many days. "These are Thy servants and Thy people, O Lord. Let now thine ear be attentive to their prayers as they desire to honor Thy name. Please prosper me also and grant me mercy in the sight of the king" (see Nehemiah 1:10–11).

One day while performing his duties, the king asked Nehemiah why his countenance was so sad. "There must be sorrow in your heart, since you are not sick." Nehemiah replied, "Why should not my countenance be sad when the city of my fathers' sepulchers [graves], lies waste, and the city gates have been consumed with fire?" (Neh. 2:3). King Artaxerxes was receptive to what Nehemiah told him; his heart was softened, and he asked: "What do you wish me to do?" This was the opportunity that Nehemiah had prayed for. "If it pleases you and I have found favor in your sight, I would have you send me to Judah, to the city of my fathers that I may rebuild it." The king inquired as to when Nehemiah wanted to leave and how long he expected to be gone. Nehemiah proposed a timeframe which was acceptable to the king. In addition, Nehemiah asked, "If it pleases you, give me letters to the governors west of the Euphrates that I might have safe passage through their lands—and also a letter to the keeper of the forest that he will give me timber for the city's many gates." Shortly, Nehemiah was on his way to Jerusalem with the desired letters from the king, as well as a letter appointing him governor of Judea. The king also sent horsemen and captains from his army to accompany Nehemiah and protect him on his journey.

When Nehemiah first arrived in Jerusalem, he did not disclose why he had come. But after being in the city for three days, he went out by night to survey the city walls and assess the extent of the damage. When he returned from surveying the destruction, he met with Jewish leaders and told them: "You see how Jerusalem lies in waste and the gates are burned with fire. Come now, let us build up the walls of our city that we are no longer a disgrace." Nehemiah also told the Jewish leaders the words of King Artaxerxes—how he had been appointed governor of Judea and had been charged with rebuilding the city walls—how the hand of Jehovah had brought him to Jerusalem, they were excited and sustained the plan, declaring, "Let us rise up and build."

However, not everyone was happy with this plan. Rebuilding the city walls was not without opposition. Nehemiah's project was not popular with the governors of surrounding territories. Chief among his opponents were Sanballat the Horonite; Tobiah the Ammonite; and Geshem the Arabian. When these detractors heard of Nehemiah's plan, they despised the Jews even more than they previously had and laughed them to scorn. These men grieved exceedingly "that there was a man come seeking the welfare of the children of Judah" (Neh. 2:10). Nehemiah, fearless and undaunted in his objective, boldly told these opponents to the project that Jehovah would prosper his servants: "We will arise and build, for we have the King's blessing. And because you have no portion, no right, and no memorial in the city of Jerusalem, you have no right to tell us what we can and cannot do" (Neh. 2:17–20).

Nehemiah then organized his resources, divided the tasks of building so that various groups of men were assigned to rebuild different sections of the wall. Thus, the entire wall was being rebuilt simultaneously, and the work proceeded rapidly: "for the people had a mind to work" (Neh. 4:6). However, Sanballat was not willing to let the matter rest. In his determination to stop the work, he mocked the workers and spoke out to the Samaritan army: "What will the Jews do? Will they fortify themselves with stones from rubbish heaps?" Tobiah joined in the mocking of Jewish builders with his sarcastic comments: "The quality of the work is poor. If a fox were to go up this wall that they are building, the fox's weight would break it down." Undaunted, the workers continued to build despite the ridiculing and taunting.

But as the walls of the city continued to rise, opposition intensified. Nehemiah's enemies conspired and hatched plans to do battle against Jerusalem and tear down walls that had been partially rebuilt. The threats were very real; and they grew so intimidating that Nehemiah confessed, "They make us afraid" (Neh. 6:9). But with much encouragement in his voice, Nehemiah pleaded: "Do not fear our enemies. Trust in Jehovah, who is great and revered; then fight for your brethren, your sons, your daughters, your wives, and your houses." The vindictive plot was discovered and those who had hatched it knew that Jehovah had brought their evil counsel to naught. Workers returned to their labors with renewed energy. From that time forth, half the men worked, and the other half stood guard. Every man labored, as it were, with one hand, while holding a weapon in the other. Those with homes outside Jerusalem no longer left the city at night. They labored by day and stood guard by night to protect the partially completed walls.

When Sanballat, Tobiah, and Geshem learned that there were no longer any breaches in the city wall, they requested on four different occasions that Nehemiah come out to meet them at a village located on the plain of Ono. However, Nehemiah discerned that the motive of the three leaders was to lure him out of the city and harm him in some way. Each time that He was approached about meeting with the three leaders of the opposition, he responded to their message with the same answer:

"I will not come out; I am doing a great work, so I cannot come down." (Nehemiah 6:3)

What a remarkable response, reflecting his unlimited *hope* to see the city walls of Jerusalem rebuilt! What a clear and unchanging purpose of heart and mind! Undeterred, the three leaders concocted a devious scheme after the four attempts to convince Nehemiah to meet with them had failed. Sanballat penned a letter full of allegations: "It has been reported that the Jews seek to rebel against King Artaxerxes and that you are building this wall so that you can become king. It is also reported that you have appointed prophets who are preaching to the people that you will be the king of Judah. If you do not come and counsel with us, we will report these matters to Artaxerxes." Furious at such accusations, and knowing that this was, in essence, blackmail. Nehemiah sent his reply: "There are no such things being done. You have only imagined them in your hearts." Once again, the nefarious plan of the three leaders was foiled. Building continued. With tremendous, unwavering commitment, the walls and gates of Jerusalem were rebuilt in an astonishing fifty-two days (Neh. 6:15).[6]

Our hope is for the triumphal arrival of Jesus Christ in His glorious Second Coming. Preparing for it involves "a great work and we cannot come down" from our scaffolding wherein we are constructing a Zion people ready and worthy to receive Him in His glory.

Hope vs. Optimism

"Hope" and "optimism" are *not* the same thing. The optimist looks at the world and feels good about the way things are going. Things are looking up! Everything is going to be all right! But hope, at least conceived within the Jewish and then the early Christian world, was quite different. Hope could be, and often was, a dogged and deliberate choice when the world seemed dark. It depended not on a *feeling* about the way things were or the way they were moving, but on *faith*, faith in the One True God—the God who had created the earth. This God had called Israel to be His people. The scriptures, not the least being Psalms (which in the hierarchy of Jewish theological liturgy ranks number two right after Deuteronomy) makes it abundantly clear that God could be trusted to sort things out in the end, and would be true to His promises and covenants to redeem His people, even if it had to be after terrible suffering and testing.

The strains of a favorite hymn ring with clarity in our ears, are emblazoned on our souls, and are written on our hearts. We rejoice as we sing, "There is hope smiling brightly before us, and we know that deliverance is nigh" ("We Thank Thee O God for a Prophet," *Hymns*, no. 19). You, the reader, are no doubt familiar with the miraculous events involving Saul (Aramaic, later Paul, which is Roman) on the road to Damascus. In looking at this pivotal encounter, it is illuminating to take what we know of Saul *before* the appearance of Christ compared to what we know of him *after* the vision occurs and place these contrasting portraits within the rich cultural and spiritual Jewish world of Paul's day, replete as it was with various forms of the controlling Jewish narrative. We must look carefully to see what emerges about the way in which the "zeal" of the eager young Torah student emerged in a different form as "zeal" for the good news, aka the *evangelion*, the gospel, the message about Jesus—the fulfillment, shocking as it seemed, of the ancestral hope of the Jews. Some saw it, at the time, as have many since, as one narrative replacing another. The word "conversion" itself has often been taken that way. But Saul—Paul the Apostle—saw it as the same narrative, now, however, demanding to be understood in a radical, but justifiable new way. The narrative in question was the hope of Israel. If we were to assert that Saul was brought up in a world of hope, many have and do misunderstand.

Hope in this sense is not a feeling. It is a virtue. It is built on the foundation of faith in Jesus Christ. We must practice at it, like learning a difficult piece on a musical instrument, for instance. We practice the virtue of hope through worship and prayer, invoking God through reading and deeply thinking the scriptural narratives, and through consciously viewing the unknown future through the lenses of unshakable divine promises. In Paul's world, those unshakable promises (covenants) were focused on one great story, with one singular element that would make all the difference. That great story was the ancient freedom story, the Passover narrative, but with a new twist—namely, the Crucifixion and Resurrection of Jesus Christ, which fulfilled the Abrahamic covenant and rescued the human family from exile and bondage. The Way became a culture, a movement, suffused with hope. This is the great message which now emerged from Paul's preaching of the gospel throughout the Mediterranean basin. Hope engulfed the heads and hearts of Paul and the other early missionaries, including the Twelve.

That story gave shape and energy to their aspirations and motivations. It explains both hope and action in Paul's life as it should in ours. What is that narrative? Christ crucified and resurrected will come again in great glory and power to rule and reign here on earth for a thousand years. And Satan the unrelenting enemy of the story will be bound and not able to interfere with or impede the process of (a) proclaiming the fullness of the gospel of *hope* to all of the family of Heavenly Father; (b) enabling those who wish to enter into the salvific covenants of the Gospel—namely, baptism, and those consummated in the temple—to do so; (c) releasing those souls in spirit prison, including those temporarily consigned to hell (Official Declaration 1). Each soul will be taught the doctrines of the gospel and given full opportunity to accept or reject its message of redemption to those who adopt and incorporate the "Faith, Hope, Charity Triad" in their lives by accepting Christ as the Son of God, the Messiah, the Redeemer, and the Father of our Heavenly Father's children who honor the covenants made available to them.

Notes

1. Attributed to Bill Frey, from a sermon preached at the Trinity School for Ministry, Ambridge, PA, September 2001, as quoted in Kenneth E. Bailey, *Paul through Mediterranean Eyes* (Downers Grove, IL: InterVarsity Press, 2011), 477.
2. C. S. Lewis, *Christian Behaviour* (London: Macmillan, 1943), 55; emphasis added.
3. Neal A. Maxwell, "Hope through the Atonement of Jesus Christ," *Ensign*, November 1998; emphasis added.
4. Dieter F. Uchtdorf, "The Infinite Power of Hope," *Ensign*, November 2008; emphasis added.
5. Thomas S. Monson, "Courage Counts," *Ensign*, November 1986.
6. Adapted from Val D. Greenwood, *How Often I Would Have Gathered You: Stories from the Old Testament and Related Sources* (Salt Lake City: Millennial Publishing, 2007), 317–19.

Chapter 14

Scriptures = Super Vitamins

"These words are not of men . . . but of me . . .
For it is my *voice* which speaketh them unto you . . .
and by my power you can read them to one another . . .
wherefore you can testify that you have *heard* my voice."
(D&C 18:34-36)

"The thing which impresses me about these verses is, and I
had never thought of it before,
when I read this verse, I am hearing the voice
of the Lord as well as reading His words."
(S. Dilworth Young)[1]

It is just too irresistible to not put some CPA terminology in this text. So here goes! Just as Lehi was told that one of the purposes for taking a set of scriptures with him to the promised land—namely, that without them, his posterity would dwindle in unbelief—we should feel deep gratitude and have an enormous feeling of joy that we have four books of scripture comprising our standard works—not just one. We can read so many of God's words that He has spoken to His children. What a marvelous blessing! The scriptures are super-vitamins designed for energy to walk the covenant path.

Less Is More

Mark Twain once observed, "A successful book is not made of what is in it; but what is left out of it."[2] Based on that criterion, the Book of Mormon would be a wildly successful piece of literature. That sacred record is replete with things which are *not* there, from such cultural details as to what Nephite cities looked like to the far more personal details—relationships, biographical data, emotions, questions, etc. The text exhibits overwhelming evidence of having been carefully crafted; the narrators (Nephi, Alma 2, and Mormon) picking and choosing what is best left to our imaginations. Robert Alter echoed this theme relative to the Bible:

> How does the Bible manage to evoke such a sense of depth and complexity in its representation of character with what would seem to be such sparse, even rudimentary means? Biblical narrative offers us, after all, nothing in the way of minute analysis of motive or detailed rendering of mental processes; whatever indication we may be vouchsafed of feeling, attitude, or intention are rather minimal; and we are given only the barest hints about the physical appearance, the tics and gestures, the dress and implements of the characters, the material milieu in which they enact their destinies. In short, all of the indicators of nuanced individuality to which the Western literary tradition has accustomed us—preeminently in the novel, but ultimately going back to the Greek epics and romances—would appear to be absent from the Bible. . . .
>
> . . . Though biblical narrative is often silent where later modes of fiction choose to be loquacious, *it is selectively silent in a purposeful way.*[3]

Rather than lamenting that we do not have multitudinous details about Book of Mormon peoples, culture, events, and places, because they apparently are not important to our salvation, perhaps it would be more accurate and useful to say that the narrators did not include them in the text because *not* knowing them may be *more* significant to our salvation. While the text does reveal special glimpses into fascinating characters like Nephi, Amulek, Alma, among others, we are being invited to learn much more about ourselves. Lack of details makes it easier for us to relate to the Book of Mormon characters.

For example, most Latter-day Saints cannot (and would not want to) relate very well to Alma the Younger. Most of us have not purposely tried to destroy the Church and wage all-out persecution against the members thereof, and then endure three days in a coma, going through the process of repentance. Amulek, however, is a different situation. Many of us have felt, at times, that we have fallen short in how we serve. Many may also believe, as did Amulek, that they have been called, but would not hear; that we knew, but would not know (see Alma 10:5–6). If the narrator had made it clear exactly what Amulek was referring to, then perhaps fewer readers would see themselves in him. But since we really do not know how far Amulek had strayed from the covenant path, the narrator leads us to ask questions of ourselves and our location relative to the covenant path. We reflect on how well we have heard the voice of the Lord, on how hesitant we may have been sometimes to admit that we know what we know.

Another example is Nephi, who laments: "O wretched man that I am! Yea, my heart sorroweth because of my flesh; my soul grieveth because of mine iniquities" (2 Nephi 4:17). As with Amulek, we can relate to the circumstances surrounding Nephi's Psalm. Once again, there are no details as to the sources of or causes for what Nephi considers his "wretchedness" and his iniquities." I assert that omitting details concerning Nephi and Amulek is not accidental. Had specific details of what it was that gave Nephi and Amulek reason to lament and repent, there would certainly be more than a trivial temptation for us to measure ourselves against the rulers of Nephi's "wretchedness" and Amulek's "shortcomings." Indulging in comparative unrighteousness is not conducive to progress along the covenant path. The only measuring rod for our lives is the "rod of Jesse," which was prophesied by Isaiah in predicting the advent of Jesus Christ in the meridian of time (see Isaiah 11:1).

For a Wiser Purpose

We are all familiar with the "lost 116 manuscript pages" narrative and surrounding circumstances, so I will not recount the details here. Elder Jeffrey R. Holland offers us insight and comfort regarding the lost 116 pages, representing the efforts of Joseph's initial translation work of the golden plates:

> At least six times in the Book of Mormon, the phrase "for a wise purpose" is used in reference to making, writing, and preserving

the small plates of Nephi . . . We know one such wise purpose—the most obvious one—was to compensate for the future loss of 116 pages of manuscript translated. . . .

But it strikes me that there is a *"wiser purpose"* than that . . . the key to such a suggestion is in Doctrine and Covenants 10:45. ["Behold, there are many things engraven upon the plates of Nephi which do throw *greater views* upon my gospel" (emphasis added).] . . .

So clearly this was not a *quid pro quo* in the development of the final Book of Mormon product. It was not tit for tat, this for that—116 pages of manuscript for 142 pages of printed text. No so. We got back more than we lost. And it was known from the beginning that it would be so. We do not know exactly what we have missed in the lost 116 pages, but we do know that what we received on the small plates was the personal declarations [about having seen Jesus Christ] of three great witnesses [Nephi, Jacob and Isaiah], three of the great doctrinal voices of the Book of Mormon testifying that Jesus is the Christ.[4]

Being taught by Elder Holland that the small plates of Nephi "throw greater views upon my gospel" could not result in any clearer message that the scriptures, especially the Book of Mormon, are super-vitamins that are to be taken every day. Some Saints naively assert that there is nothing "new" that can be found after reading the scriptures a couple of times. But to me knowing that there are "greater views" to be had concerning the gospel is sufficient to warrant reading in them every day. And to continue reading them again and again. About the time that I begin thinking that there is really nothing that I can learn from reading the Book of Mormon another time is when I discover something different that I had not previously seen. I mentioned in the preface that my gospel education class had just spent more than two and a half years rediscovering the Book of Mormon. I cannot tell you how many "greater views" emerged from that deep dive. God's words are inexhaustible. Read them again and again. President Benson made this significant observation:

However diligent we may be in other areas [of gospel living], *certain blessings are to be found only in the scriptures.*[5]

C. S. Lewis ratifies and further alludes to the importance of scriptures as we navigate our mortal journey:

> Domesticity is no passport to heaven on earth but an arduous vocation—a sea full of hidden rocks and perilous ice shores only to be navigated by one who uses a celestial chart [the scriptures].[6]

We find tremendous assurance from things that prophets have said in the scriptures. For instance, Paul writes, "We look not at the things which are seen, but at the things which are not seen" (2 Corinthians 4:18). Elder Neil L. Andersen ratified that Paul's comment: "We have the responsibility to teach our Creator's plan for His children and to warn of the consequences of disregarding His commandments."[7] Elder Bednar adds:

> A farmer cannot expect to harvest in the fall if he does not properly sow in the spring and work hard during the summer to weed, nourish, and cultivate the field. So it is for you and me. We cannot expect to reap scriptural insight unless we pay the price of regular and diligent study. Casual strolling through or dabbling in the scriptures will not yield enduring gospel understanding.[8]

The scriptures are replete with blessings from our Father in Heaven. Our joyful task is to search them out, and like panning for gold, find those golden nuggets of salvation. Some day we will have access to "what was not in" the Bible, Book of Mormon, book of Moses, and the book of Abraham. They will be available in the Lord's timing. Let's take a couple of patience vitamins and ponder the possible meanings of things we don't yet have.

"He Restoreth My Soul" (Psalms 23:3)

The caption for this section needs no introduction. It is universally recognized as one of the key lines in David's Psalm 23. Many have written about the "restoring" process with the consensus being that this symbolic phrase has particular reference to the Sabbath. I would propose a different methodology by which the Shepherd restores souls. I will preface my thoughts on the subject of "He restoreth my soul" by sharing a story I once read involving a group of tourists on safari in Africa in a book by Harold S. Kushner:

> They had hired several native porters to carry their supplies while they trekked. After three days, the porters told them that they would have to stop and rest for a day. They were not tired, they explained, but "we have walked too far too fast and now we must wait for our souls to catch up to us." We too can be so busy taking care of things that we neglect our souls.[9]

The world asks so much of us. We give ourselves to our work, to the endless task of raising our family, running a home, career advancement to our volunteer commitments, etc. The list goes on as far as the eye can see. We often forget to take time to let Christ, the Good Shepherd, nourish and *restore* our souls, forgetting that we need to replenish and rely on the "wisdom of the soul" (a.k.a., the scriptures) to guide our working and living hours.

I assert that, in addition to resting on Shabbat, we study the scriptures to have our souls restored. Kushner continues:

> The prophet Jeremiah compares the person who scorns and rejects God to a tree planted in the desert, which will ultimately dry up and wither because it has no source of replenishment outside itself, while "he who trusts the Lord . . . shall be like a tree planted by waters . . . its leaves are ever fresh, it has not care in a year of drought, it does not cease to bear fruit" (Jeremiah 17:7-8). When we are emotionally empty, we are not able to replenish ourselves. The restoration, the replenishment, has to come from somewhere outside ourselves, from God and from people inspired by God to reach out to us in our need.[10]

There is another image in Psalm 23 to keep in mind: "my cup runneth over." Once we have learned to recognize that our lives are a reflection of accumulated gifts that God has abundantly given us from having restored ourselves by studying His word; and once we have learned to appreciate what we have, rather than complain that we don't have more, because we could have had nothing, there are two things we should do in response. First, we reciprocate God's generosity for sharing with us "all

151

that He has revealed, and all that He does now reveal and [with hopeful anticipation] all that He will yet reveal" (Articles of Faith 1:9) by expressing our sincere gratitude and our trust that He "restores" us again and again. Second, when we discover that our cup runs over with God's abundance, our response should be to request and obtain a bigger cup. Our ability to enjoy and absorb God's blessing of pouring out knowledge is more a function of our capacity to receive knowledge than of any limitations on God's ability to reveal knowledge to us which pertains to the kingdom of God. Truly, spending time each day to restore our souls and allowing God to enlarge our cup will be well worth the effort.

I am reminded of the Old Testament story of the widow's oil found in 2 Kings 4. The widow of Obadiah, the God-fearing steward of King Ahab's (approx. 900 BC) house, sought out Elisha the Prophet seeking his counsel.

> She explains her dilemma: "My husband feared [loved] Jehovah, but he is now dead, and his creditor is threatening to take my two sons as bondsmen."
>
> Elisha asks, "How would you have me help you? Tell me what you have in your house."
>
> The widow replies, "I have nothing of value in my house except one pot of oil."
>
> To which Elisha advised her, "Go then, and borrow as many empty vessels as you can from your neighbors. Once you have them, go into your house and shut the door. Then you and your sons should take your pot of oil and pour it into all those vessels and set each vessel aside when it is full."
>
> Trusting Elisha's words, the widow gathers empty vessels from her neighbors, and shuts the door behind herself and her two sons. As her sons bring the empty vessels to her, the widow pours oil from her vessel which poured without interruption. When all the vessels were full, she asks her sons to bring another vessel. Her sons reply that there are no more vessels. And at that point the supply of oil ceases to increase.

Not knowing what to do next, the widow returns to Elisha and tells him what happened and how all the vessels she collected from her neighbors had all been filled.

Elisha then instructs her to "Go, sell enough oil to pay your debt; then you and your sons shall live on the rest." (See 2 Kings 4:1–7)

The word of the Lord will flow without interruption and fill our souls—we just need to present a larger cup to Him. Wonderfully, the Lord makes our cups larger when we involve Him in the process through meaningful prayer, which includes listening to the Holy Ghost.

"Nor Ever Before Had Thought Of"

Let us recall the "before and after" experience of Joseph Smith, who speaks of reading the scriptures *after* receiving the Holy Ghost. He was astonished, looking back and comparing his post-Holy Ghost reading experiences with his pre-Holy Ghost readings. He illuminates us:

> Our minds [his and Oliver Cowdery's] being now enlightened, we began to have the scriptures laid open to our understandings, and the true meaning *and intention of their more mysterious [sacred] passages* revealed unto us in a manner we never could attain to previously, *nor ever before had thought of.* (Joseph Smith—History 1:74; emphasis added)

Imagine that! We can grasp the "intentions" of the more mysterious (sacred) passages in the inspiration revealed to the prophets and recorded by them. How can that be a blessing to us? Recall, for example, what Lehi prophesied in his patriarchal blessing to his young son Joseph, just prior to his death:

> But a seer [Joseph Smith] will I raise up out of the fruit of thy loins; and unto him will I give power to bring forth my word [the Book of Mormon] unto the seed of thy loins—and not to the bringing forth my word only, saith the Lord, *but to the convincing them of my word [the Bible], which shall have already gone forth among them.* (2 Nephi 3:11; emphasis added)

Lehi's prophecy explicitly states that we are to use the Book of Mormon to prove the Bible, rather than using the Holy Bible to prove the Book of Mormon. When we utilize the Book of Mormon in preference to the Holy Bible in teaching the restored gospel to those not of our faith tradition, it has the effect of removing us from the arena of argument over the meaning of biblical texts. Joseph figured out this "missionary concept" pretty quickly as he laments: "The teachers of religion . . . understood the same passages of scripture so differently as to destroy all confidence in settling the question by an appeal to the Bible" (Joseph Smith—History 1:12). President Ezra Taft Benson adds another important dimension to the importance of our need to study the scriptures:

> We therefore should know the Book of Mormon better than any other book. Not only should we know what history and faith-promoting stories it contains, but we should understand its teachings. . . . I have noted within the Church a difference in discernment, insight, conviction, and spirit between those who know and love the Book of Mormon and those who do not. *That book is a great sifter.*[11]

President Dieter F. Uchtdorf, second counselor in the First Presidency (at the time), was the keynote speaker at the 2012 BYU Church History Symposium and drew his theme from a quoted remark made by novelist Michael Crichton: "If you don't know history, you don't know anything. You are a leaf that doesn't know it is part of a tree."[12] Then President Uchtdorf added this insight:

> History teaches us not only about the leaves of existence; it also teaches about the twigs, branches, trunks, and roots of life. And these lessons are important.
>
> One of the weaknesses we have as mortals is to assume that *our "leaf"* is all there is—that our experience encompasses everyone else's, that our truth is complete and universal. . . .
>
> . . . Heavenly Father teaches His children over and again not to place their trust in the wisdom of the world. . . . Yet we have

an almost irresistible desire to assume that our leaf of information we have in our possession is a representation of all there is to know.[13]

Studying the scriptures enables us to see the whole tree—not just an individual leaf, which perhaps, is something "nor ever before [we] thought of."

Great Are the Words of Isaiah

There is probably no more formidable book within the canon of Latter-day Saint scripture than the book of Isaiah as found in the Old Testament along with the numerous passages quoted in the Book of Mormon, particularly those found in 2 Nephi. To encourage those of us who tremble at the prospect of reading, let alone studying, Isaiah, may I offer some suggestions that might help make the vitamin pill go down. First, let's see what Nephi says: "In the days that the prophecies of Isaiah shall be fulfilled [and we know that those "days" are upon us], men [and women] shall *know* of a surety, at the times when they shall come to pass. Wherefore, they are of worth unto the children of men . . . *for in that day shall they understand them*" (2 Nephi 25:7–8; emphasis added). Two important principles emerge here which provide us confidence and assurance that we can successfully study and comprehend Isaiah.

#1 We will recognize and know that the prophecies of Isaiah are being fulfilled in our day.

Even though much of Isaiah's prophetic imagery relates to the culture and time in which he lived, we can initially grasp partial meanings that will become more understandable as we become more familiar with his style and vernacular.

#2 We have been promised that we shall understand them.

Therefore, with those two keys firmly in our minds, here are some suggestions as to how to enhance our understanding of Isaiah.

- Utilize our understanding of the plan of salvation that we are taught both in the scriptures and in the temple. Relate Isaiah's writings to the doctrine of premortal existence (2 Nephi 24:12); consider the life, ministry, and Atonement of the Savior (Mosiah 14:10); and apply our understanding of the nature of and events surrounding the millennial day (2 Nephi 21:6).
- Study the doctrine of the gathering of Israel, particularly the writings of Moses in the Old Testament, and the revelations in our dispensation to the Prophet Joseph Smith.
- Study the Book of Mormon. It is our greatest scriptural commentary on Isaiah. Elder Bruce R. McConkie drove home this notion: "May I be so bold as to affirm that no one, absolutely no one, in this age and dispensation has or does or can understand the writings of Isaiah until he first learns and believes what God revealed by the mouths of his Nephite witnesses as these truths are found in that volume of holy writ [the Book of Mormon]."[14]
- Use modern-day revelations. Study the Doctrine and Covenants, which contains quotes or language from thirty-one chapters of Isaiah.
- Sermons found in the *Teachings of the Prophet Joseph Smith* contain explanations or commentary on thirty-five Isaiah passages representing portions of twenty-one chapters of Isaiah.
- Learn how New Testament authors—John the Revelator and Paul—quoted Isaiah. Read the passages quoted by the Savior in both the old and new worlds.
- Become acquainted with the manner and pattern in which Old Testament prophecies may be fulfilled. For instance, in the October 2001 General Conference, President Hinckley firmly declared that the prophecy in Joel 2:28–29, which the Angel Moroni quoted to Joseph Smith three times the night of September 23, 1823, has been fulfilled.
- Seek the spirit of prophecy through sincere prayer and devote ourselves to serious study. Recall the guidance provided by Nephi: "Nevertheless they are plain unto all those that are filled with the spirit of prophecy" (2 Nephi 25:4).
- Supplement scripture study with the aid of a good Isaiah commentary, of which there are several.

- The following represents a topical guide that might assist you in your study of 2 Nephi 12–24.

> 2 Nephi 12 = The building of temples in the last days
> 2 Nephi 13 = The fruits of wickedness are everlastingly the same
> 2 Nephi 14 = The day of millennial splendor
> 2 Nephi 15 = The latter-day restoration of the gospel
> 2 Nephi 16 = Isaiah's call to the ministry
> 2 Nephi 17 & 18 = Salvation cannot be found in worldly alliances
> 2 Nephi 19 = Christ to sit upon David's throne
> 2 Nephi 20 = The Lord chastens His people
> 2 Nephi 21 & 22 = Isaiah prophecies of Joseph Smith
> 2 Nephi 23 & 24 = The day of the Lord's triumph

Nephi and Jacob took the time to engrave the words of Isaiah on the gold plates for at least two reasons: (1) they knew that they would become important to their posterity, particularly the Lamanites, in recommitting to the promises made to the fathers, and (2) they were inspired by the Lord to include portions of Isaiah's writings for our benefit. Therefore, chocolate-covered vitamins will help us overcome our trepidation of Isaiah. We can also take Isaiah 401 during the Millennium!

Discovering Treasures in Language

Scholars predominantly agree that the books now comprising the New Testament were written between AD 50 (Mark and Paul's epistles being the earliest) and AD 100 (the Gospel of John and Revelations being the latest). Given this timeframe, it is no surprise that the earliest manuscripts (which are copies of copies of the original autographs, none of which we currently have ever found) were written in Greek—it being the language of the Roman Empire from 360 BC to AD 300. Since the New Testament was the scripture accompanying *Come Follow Me* for home-centered, Church-supported gospel study in 2019, I found myself with a keen interest when reading the New Testament books of looking at key words and their Greek origins. In no way did I become a Greek linguist, but I did find, on more than one occasion, a deepened understanding and different perspective to think about as I considered how words and phrases were translated from Greek into the King James Bible (KJV), the New Revised Standard Version (NRSV); the Wayment Translations (WT); and the New Oxford Annotated Bible. Among the words which grabbed my attention was "faith" since it is frequently found in the books of the New Testament.

It turns out that the Greek word used for faith is *pistis* and was usually translated that way. As mentioned several times earlier in this book, we have learned that words can mean something different in our twenty-first-century world than they did in Joseph Smith's nineteenth-century world and in the first-century world of Jesus and His followers, including Paul. So, I keep handy a copy of Webster's 1828 Dictionary (WD 1828) and regularly consult it to see what words meant in society's conversation back then. I looked up "faith" in WD 1828 and found that the most common definition of faith was "trust." This led me to look up the definition of "trust" in WD 1828. I was delighted to see the following six definitions, in order of preferential usage:

- Confidence, a resilience or resting the mind on integrity, veracity, justice, and friendship or sound principle of another person
- Confidence of something present or future
- Special reliance on honesty
- Credulous / credulity
- Rely on
- Depend on

So, whenever I encountered the word "faith" in any particular passage that I might be reading from the New Testament, I substituted the word "trust" and pondered on its meanings listed above. In many cases, a whole new and previously unconsidered understanding filled my mind. I reached the conclusion that "trust" actually conveys something deeper and more meaningful than the word "faith." In a certain sense, trust seems to be a stronger word than faith particularly as I thought about phrases (after substituting the word "trust" for "faith") such as "trust in God," "trust in the power of the Atoning sacrifice of Jesus Christ," "trust in the everlasting gospel," trust associated with keeping covenants, trust that the covenant path is the only way, etc. *Pistis* is just one example of deepening our understanding of the scriptures by looking for and considering alternative translations from the Greek.

This same technique produces similar results when studying the Old Testament and digging into the Hebrew words from which it was translated. Perhaps that is one reason we now have an "extra" hour of home-centered learning on the Sabbath! We need not be academic scholars to read the scriptures carefully, to think about them in depth, and to continue to learn from them. It is important that we not leave it solely to scholars to think deeply about the scriptures for us. An "amateur" is, etymologically, "one who loves." We amateurs, who love the scriptures, ought to be engaged in delving into them carefully, as well as lovingly, and discovering the treasures therein.

Hearing Him!

Elder Robert D. Hales puts a capstone on the truths discussed above and declares that feasting upon the scriptures is the means of hearing the voice of the Lord in our lives:

> If we don't have the word of God or don't cling to and heed the word of God, we will wander off in strange paths and be lost as individuals, as families, and as nations.
>
> As with voices from the dust, the prophets of the Lord cry out to us on earth today: take hold of the scriptures! Cling to them, walk by them, live by them, rejoice in them, and feast on them. Don't nibble. They are "the power of God unto salvation" (D&C 68:4) that lead us back to our Savior Jesus Christ.
>
> If the Savior were among us in the flesh today, He would teach us from the scriptures as He taught when He walked upon the earth. . . . His words ring out: "Search the scriptures; for . . . they are they which testify of me" (John 5:39). . . . What a glorious blessing! For when we want to speak to God, we pray. *And when we want Him to speak to us, we search the scriptures; for His words are spoken through His prophets.* He will then teach us as we listen to the promptings of the Holy Spirit.[15]

I have long held the belief that we as a people have not been given more of the records and books which God has caused to be written by peoples around the world because we have not appreciated and absorbed what we have already been given. I know that I am (as are you) anxiously awaiting the opportunity to read and study more scripture, which I hope will be forthcoming sooner rather than later. The scriptures enable us to "Hear Him" because they consist of hearing what has already been spoken and will better prepare us to receive and understand what He has spoken and is recorded on books and records, which God is anxiously awaiting to reveal to us.

Notes

1. S. Dilworth Young, in Conference Report, April 1963.
2. Mark Twain, *Mark Twain's Letters*, vol. 2, arr. Albert Bigelow Paine (New York: Harper & Brothers, 1917), 644.
3. Robert Alter, *The Art of Biblical Narrative*, rev. ed. (New York: Basic Books, 2011), 143–44; emphasis added.
4. Jeffrey R. Holland, "For a Wise Purpose," *Ensign*, January 1996.
5. Ezra Taft Benson, "The Power of the Word," *Ensign*, May 1986; emphasis added.
6. C. S. Lewis, "The Sermon and the Lunch," in *The Grand Miracle: And Other Selected Essays on Theology and Ethics from God in the Dock*, ed. Walter Hooper (New York: Ballantine Books, 1970), 163.
7. Neil L. Andersen, "Spiritual Whirlwinds," *Ensign*, May 2014.
8. David A. Bednar, "Understanding the Importance of Scripture Study" (Ricks College devotional, January 6, 1998), byui.edu.
9. Harold S. Kushner, *The Lord Is My Shepherd: Healing Wisdom of the Twenty-Third Psalm* (New York: Alfred A. Knopf, 2003), 60.
10. Kushner, 60.
11. Ezra Taft Benson, "Jesus Christ—Gifts and Expectations," *Ensign*, December 1988; emphasis added.
12. Michael Crichton, *Timeline* (New York: Knopf, 1999), 73.
13. Dieter F. Uchtdorf, "Seeing Beyond the Leaf," *Religious Educator* 15, no. 3 (2014); emphasis added.
14. Bruce R. McConkie "Ten Keys to Understanding Isaiah," *Ensign*, October 1973.
15. Robert D. Hales, "Holy Scriptures: The Power of God unto Our Salvation," *Ensign*, November 2006; emphasis added.

Chapter 15
Conclusion

The worth of a human soul
is its capacity to become as God.
(Paul C. Child)[1]

When all is said and done, our penultimate "seatbelt" and "supply of vitamins" is the Lord Jesus Christ. From the defining moment during the Grand Council in heaven, when in response to the Father's query, "Whom shall I send?" (Abraham 3:27), He resoundingly declared, "Here am I, send me," deliverance from bondage and the redemption process began. In our pre-earthly existence, the powers of Christ's atoning sacrifice were taught to us and made manifest as the spirit children who voluntarily exercised their agency and "shouted for joy" (Job 38:7) which I am sure was a Hosanna Shout. As explained by Alma, those who choose to covenant with the Father to adopt and abide by the great plan of happiness and salvation strapped on their seatbelts and ate lots of vitamins:

> And this is the manner after which they were ordained—being called and prepared from the foundation of the world according to the foreknowledge of God, *on account of their exceeding faith and good works;* in the first place being left to *choose good or evil;* therefore they having chosen good, and *exercising exceedingly great faith,* are called with a holy calling, yea, with that holy call which was *prepared with and according to, a preparatory redemption for such.* (Alma 13:3; emphasis added)

How that "preparatory redemption" was operational in pre-earth life we are not told—all we know is that the Savior's ministry to save all of Father's children began and continues today in that premortal world as well as here on our earthly home. After Adam and Eve knowingly made the choice to become mortal and begin life on this earth, Jesus taught them the gospel's plan, whereupon Eve rejoiced:

> And Eve . . . heard all these things and was glad, saying: Were it not for our transgression we never should have had seed, and never should have known good and evil, and the joy of our redemption, and the eternal life which God giveth unto all the obedient. (Moses 5:11)

After the children of Israel rejected the fulness of the gospel as had been practiced since the days of Adam and Eve, who had "made all things known unto their sons and their daughters" (Moses 5:12), Jesus, manifesting himself as Yahweh, instituted the law of Moses to be the "schoolmaster to bring us unto Christ" (Galatians 3:24). Then He restored and taught the fulness of the gospel during and after His thirty-three-year mortal experience declaring Himself the Messiah of Israel to household of Judah in Jerusalem—the branch (descendants of Lehi) planted in another part of the Lord's vineyard, and then to the posterity of the Ten Tribes of Israel along with others of Abraham's posterity who had been dispersed among all nations. Finally, to inaugurate the dispensation of the fulness of times, the Father and the Son appeared to the Prophet Joseph Smith and initiated the Restoration of all things which will continue until Christ's glorious Second Coming. It is overwhelming and beyond full comprehension to ponder the magnificence and glory of the Father's plan.

Before this earth was organized, the three members of the Godhead prepared and executed an everlasting covenant that would govern their joint ministry to mortals. God, finding He was in the midst of spirits and because He was more intelligent than them all, saw proper to institute laws that would operate through covenants whereby all His children could have the privilege to advance like Himself. The Council of Gods extended the possibility of a covenant relationship with the entire human family so that in our weakness we might be lifted up and exalted through the Atonement of Jesus Christ by our faithfulness in honoring our covenant with them. This relationship we have with God places us in a situation to progress through eternity in knowledge so that we might be exalted with Him.

> For the Father, and the Son, and the Holy Spirit with good fellowship and right good will and cordial agreement together made the Heavenly Zion to be the place of habitation of their Glory. And then the Father and the Son, and the Holy Spirit said, "Let Us make man [male and female] in Our similitude and likeness," and with ready agreement and goodwill they were each of this opinion. And the Son said, "I will put on the body of Adam," and the Holy Spirit said, "I will dwell in the heart[s] of the Prophets and the Righteous," and this common agreement and covenant was [fulfilled] in Zion, the City of their Glory.[2]

Continuing along this line of thought about the significant events in which we participated in our pre-earth life, Elder John A. Widtsoe enlightens us further, as paraphrased by scholar Jeffrey M. Bradshaw:

> Our premortal covenants established a partnership with God, enabling us to join with Him in the great collaborative process of salvation and exaltation. . . . All premortal souls [who sustained God's plan] similarly expressed their willingness to make sacrifices in order to advance the happiness and salvation of others.[3]

It is abundantly clear and cannot be misunderstood in any way that in our premortal state, in the day of the Great Council, we made covenants with the Almighty. The Father presented His plan of happiness. Note that there was only one plan presented. It is a Mormon myth that Lucifer also presented a plan. A closer look at Abraham 3:27–28 reveals that what occurred is that "another answered and said: Here am I, send me. And the Lord said: I will send the first. And the second was angry, and kept not his first estate [meaning that Lucifer chose not to make any covenants associated with the plan] and, at that day, many followed after him."

We accepted and rejoiced in the plan; it was intended for all men and women. We became parties to the salvation of every person under that plan. We agreed, right then and there, to be saviors not only for ourselves but for the entire human family. The execution of the plan became not merely the Father's work (see Moses 1:39) and the Savior's work, but also our work, which entails doing the "works of Abraham" (D&C 132:32). Realization of the fulness of the plan's objectives depends on covenants.

As a party to the covenant, Jesus Christ had developed an unshakable disposition to do the will of the Father and was therefore chosen to fulfill the unique and essential mission of redemption and mercy—a mission that required him to experience the greatest demands and suffering, more than all of his brothers and sisters combined (see D&C 122:8). He bore the weight of an infinite and eternal (see Alma 43:10–16 and 2 Nephi 9:5–26) atonement on our behalf. You and I as parties to the covenant received specific assignments. Each of us committed to be willing to bear the burden of whatever circumstances and challenges our Father chose to give us, being prepared when the time came to respond to the terms of the covenant and performing our appointed part in the intricate drama of salvation history. We understood that it is not only "an election to privilege, but also a responsibility."[4]

I share three morsels of wisdom—one from Elder Neal A. Maxwell, one from President Gordon B. Hinckley, and the other from President Howard W. Hunter—that focus our thoughts on the challenges which are and will continue to face us this giving rise to the need for seatbelts and vitamins in the coming days.

Elder Maxwell:

> Ironically, as the restored Church comes "out of obscurity" what seem to be stern challenges will actually disclose further distinctiveness of the Church (D&C 1:30). Nevertheless, *matching our behavior more closely with our beliefs* will bring relentless reminders about the ongoing duties of discipleship.
>
> The restored gospel is buoyant, wide, and deep—beyond our comprehension. It edifies, whether concerning divine design in the universe or stressing the importance of personal chastity and fidelity. Only *meek* disciples can safely handle *such a bold* theology.[5]

President Hinckley:

This is "the only true and living church upon the face of the whole earth" according to the word of revelation (D&C 1:30). Here lies the truth. Here lies the priesthood. Hold to the Church. Do not ever lose sight of the fact that the Church must ever remain pre-eminent in your lives if you are going to be happy as the years pass. *Never let yourselves be found in the position of fighting The Church* of Jesus Christ of Latter-day Saints. You cling to it and be faithful to it. You uphold and sustain it. You teach its doctrine and live by it. And I do not hesitate to say that your lives will be richer and the happier because of that. *You cannot find happiness fighting the work of God.* Those who have done so have gone down to a dismal end.[6]

President Hunter:

In this last dispensation there will be great tribulation. . . .

Invariably, the natural result of some of these kinds of prophecies [e.g., last days—see D&C 29 and 45] is fear, and that is not fear limited to a younger generation. It is fear shared by those of any age who don't understand. . . .

But I want to stress that these feelings are not necessary for faithful Latter-day Saints, and they do not come from God. To ancient Israel, the Great Jehovah said:

"Be strong and of a good courage, fear not, nor be afraid of them: for the Lord thy God, he it is that doth go with thee; he will not fail thee, nor forsake thee. . . .

"And the Lord, he it is that go before thee; he will be with thee, he will not fail thee, neither forsake thee: fear not, neither be dismayed." (Deut 31:6, 8)[7]

Recently the Tabernacle Choir at Temple Square performed the hymn "It Is Well with My Soul," a beloved poem written by a lawyer named Horatio Spafford in December 1873 on a ship midway between New York and London. Some years later, the poem was put to music. It is found in many Protestant hymnals and is regularly sung in churches. Moved by the choir's performance, I did some research to get the words of the hymn. That effort rewarded me with the inspirational backstory of the circumstances in Mr. Spafford's life which prompted his penning the lyrics (see below).

Spafford lived in Chicago and was a highly successful attorney and real estate developer. However, in October 1871, what has come to be known as the "Great Fire" virtually wiped out Spafford's fortune. Struggling to recover from his economic setback, Spafford and his wife, who were devout Christians of great faith, decided to relocate to Israel to start a new life. In November 1873, Spafford arranged for his wife and four daughters to travel to France on *Ville du Havre,* en route to their final destination, Jerusalem. He would conclude his business affairs in Chicago and join them in Paris as soon as he could arrange the necessary transportation. On the evening of November 23, 1873, the *Ville du Havre* inexplicably collided with the British vessel *Lochearn* and sank into the frigid waters of the North Atlantic. There were only fifty-seven survivors, half of which were crew of the *Ville du Havre.* Spafford's wife was one of the twenty-eight passengers who were rescued from the icy waters. Tragically, all four daughters drowned. When Mrs. Spafford reached Cardiff, Wales, on December 1, 1873, she sent her anxious husband—who by then had become aware of the tragedy—a now-famous telegram consisting of only two words: "Saved Alone." Crushed by the news, Spafford cabled his wife that she should travel to Paris, where she had friends including their pastor, and that he would join her as soon as possible. During his voyage across the Atlantic, the captain, who was aware of the tragic circumstances surrounding the loss of Mr. Spafford's daughters, arranged for him to be in the ship's bridge when they passed over the spot where the fateful collision had occurred. When he returned to his cabin, Spafford wrote the following lines which express my feelings about navigating the coming days.

It Is Well with My Soul

When peace like a river attendeth my way,
When sorrows like sea billows roll,
Whatever my lot, Thou hast taught me to say:
It is well, it is well with my soul.

Though Satan should buffet, though trials should come,
Let this blessed assurance control,
That Christ hath regarded my helpless estate,
And hath shed His own blood for my soul.

My sin, oh, the bliss of this glorious thought!
My sin, not in part but the whole,
Is nailed to the cross, and I bear it no more;
Praise the Lord, praise the Lord, O my soul!

And, Lord, haste the day when faith shall be sight,
The clouds be rolled back as a scroll,
The trump shall resound, and the Lord shall descend—
Even so—it is well with my soul.[8]

May God bless us through personal revelation to grasp the reality of how close we are to the Savior's Second Coming and that we are engaged in furthering His plan. May we have the humility to accept and resolutely be guided by God's words to Abraham: "I will lead thee by *my* hand." Our task is simply to buckle up them seatbelts, chow down those chocolate vitamins, and enjoy the continuing restoration of the gospel in the closing moments of the ride toward the Second Coming!

Notes

1. Paul C. Child, as quoted in Thomas S. Monson, "Tears, Trials, Trust, Testimony," *Ensign*, September 1997.

2. See Early Ethiopian Christian document, the *Kebra Nagast, The Queen of Sheba and Her Only Son Menyelek—Kebra Nagast*, 2nd ed., ed. E. A Wallis Budge (London: Oxford University Press, 1932, Reprint New York: Cosimo Classics, 2004), 1. See also John A Tvedtnes, "The King Follett Discourse in Light of Ancient and Medieval Jewish Christian Beliefs," FAIR Conference presentation, 2004, http//www.fairlds.org/pubs/2004TveJ.html.

3. John A. Widtsoe, as summarized by Jeffrey M. Bradshaw, "If 'All Are Alike Unto God,' Why Were Special Promises Reserved for Abraham's Seed?" LDSmag.com, February 11, 2018.

4. P. E. S. Thompson, "The Yahwist Creation Story," *Vestus Testamentum* 21, no. 2 (April 2, 1971): 208.

5. Neal A. Maxwell, "Encircled in the Arms of His Love," *Ensign*, November 2002; emphasis added.

6. Gordon B. Hinckley, "Excerpts from Recent Addresses of President Gordon B. Hinckley," *Ensign*, April 1966, 72–73; emphasis added.
7. Howard W. Hunter, "An Anchor to the Souls of Men," *Ensign*, October 1993.
8. As quoted in Bertha Spafford Vestor, *Our Jerusalem, an American Family in the Holy City, 1881–1949* (Garden City, NY: Doubleday & Company, 1950), 45–46. It should be noted that Bertha Spafford Vestor was born while her parents Mr. and Mrs. Horatio Spafford lived in Israel.

Bibliography

Alter, Robert. *The Art of Biblical Narrative*. Revised edition. New York: Basic Books, 2011.

The Alternative Service Book 1980. Cambridge: Cambridge University Press, 1980.

Andersen, Neil L. "Spiritual Whirlwinds." *Ensign*, May 2014.

Aurandt, Paul. *Paul Harvey's Rest of the Story*. New York: Bantam Books, 1978.

Ballard, M. Russell. "Let Us Think Straight." Brigham Young University devotional, August 20, 2013. speeches.byu.edu.

———. "Like a Flame Unquenchable." *Ensign*, May 1999.

Beck, Julie B. "And Upon the Handmaids in Those Days Will I Pour Out My Spirit." *Ensign*, May 2010.

Bednar, David A. "In the Strength of the Lord." *Ensign*, May 2017.

———. "The Tender Mercies of the Lord." *Ensign*, May 2005.

———. "Understanding the Importance of Scripture Study." Ricks College devotional, January 6, 1998. byui.edu.

Benson, Ezra Taft. *An Enemy Hath Done This*. Salt Lake City: Parliament Publishers, 1969.

———. In Conference Report, April 1969.

———. "Jesus Christ—Gifts and Expectations." *Ensign*, December 1988.

———. "The Power of the Word." *Ensign*, May 1986.

Bingham, Jean B. "United in Accomplishing God's Work." *Ensign*, May 2020.

Bradshaw, Jeffrey M. "If 'All Are Alike Unto God,' Why Were Special Promises Reserved for Abraham's Seed?" *Meridian Magazine*, February 11, 2018. ldsmag.com.

Brown, Hugh B. "Eternal Progression." Church College of Hawaii address, October 16, 1964, 8–10.

Brownson, Orestes. As quoted in David F. Holland, "Anne Hutchinson to Horace Bushnell: A New Take on the New England Sequence," *The New England Quarterly* 78, no. 2 (June 2005): 194.

Cassiodorus, Flavius Magnus Aurelius. *Institutiones*. As quoted in John Bartlett. *Familiar Quotations*. 15th edition. Boston: Little, Brown and Company, 1980.

Child, Paul C. As quoted in Thomas S. Monson. "Tears, Trials, Trust, Testimony." *Ensign*, September 1997.

Clark, J. Reuben. "To Them of the Last Wagon." In Conference Report, October 1947.

Bibliography

Conybeare, William J. and J. S. Howson. *The Life and Epistles of St. Paul*. Hartford, CT: S. S. Scranton, 1900.

Cowdery, Oliver. To Edward Partridge, Far West, Missouri, April 12, 1838. josephsmithpapers.org.

Crichton, Michael. *Timeline*. New York: Knopf, 1999.

Donne, John. "Sermon II. Preached on Christmas Eve, 1624." As quoted in *The Works of John Donne: With a Memoir of His Life*. Edited by Henry Alford. London: John W. Parker, 1839, 1:25.

Dostoyevsky, Fyodor. *The Brothers Karamazov*. Translated by Constance Garnett. New York: The Macmillan Company, 1922.

Eliot, T. S. *The Rock*. London: Faber & Faber, 1934.

Elwell, Walter A. Editor. *The Evangelical Dictionary of Theology*. Grand Rapids, MI: Baker Book House, 1984, 2001, 909.

Emerson, Ralph Waldo. "An Address Delivered before the Senior Class in Divinity College, Cambridge, Sunday Evening, 15 July, 1838." Boston: James Munroe and Company, 1838.

Evans, Richard L. Address given at the Northwest Inland Division Gathered for Zion's Camp, October 15, 1971.

Eyring, Henry B. "Face to Face with President Eyring and Elder Holland." Broadcast, March 7, 2017.

Frey, Bill. From a sermon preached at the Trinity School for Ministry, Ambridge, PA, September 2001. As quoted in Kenneth E. Bailey, *Paul through Mediterranean Eyes*. Downers Grove, IL: InterVarsity Press, 2011.

Goleman, Daniel. *Emotional Intelligence: Why It Can Matter More Than IQ*. London: Bloomsbury, 2009, 149.

Greenwood, Val D. *How Often I Would Have Gathered You: Stories from the Old Testament and Related Sources*. Salt Lake City: Millennial Publishing, 2007.

Gwilliam, Ezra. "Dear Son: Lessons from Moroni Chapter 9." *Religious Educator* 19, no. 1 (2015): 110.

Hafen, Bruce C. *The Broken Heart*. Salt Lake City: Deseret Book, 1989, 149.

Hales, Robert D. "Holy Scriptures: The Power of God unto Our Salvation." *Ensign*, November 2006.

Henley, William Ernest. "Invictus." In *Book of Verses* (1888).

Hinckley, Gordon B. "Excerpts from Recent Addresses of President Gordon B. Hinckley." *Ensign*, April 1966.

———. "The Times in Which We Live." *Ensign*, January 2002.

Holland, Jeffrey R. "Cast Not Away Thy Confidence." Brigham Young University devotional, March 2, 1999. speeches.byu.edu.

———. "For a Wise Purpose." *Ensign*, January 1996.

——— and Patricia T. Holland. *On Earth as it is in Heaven*. Salt Lake City: Deseret Book, 1989.

Hunter, Howard W. "An Anchor to the Souls of Men." *Ensign*, October 1993.

Ibn-al-Tayyib. *Sharah al-Mahriqi*. Edited by Yusif Manqariyos. 2 volumes. Egypt: al-Tawfiq Press, 1907, 2:184.

Josephus, *Antiquities* 13.5.289.

Bibliography

Joshi, Arun. "Mormon Ways of Family Life Can Resolve Conflicts in World." Paper delivered *at Ideas for the 21st Century: The Worlds of Joseph Smith*. National Taiwan University, Taipei, Taiwan. August 27, 2005.

Kreeft, Peter. *Back to Virtue*. San Francisco: Ignatius Press, 1986.

Kushner, Harold S. *The Lord I. My Shepherd: Healing Wisdom of the Twenty-Third Psalm*. New York: Alfred A. Knopf, 2003.

Lee, Harold B. In Conference Report, October 1970.

———. In Conference Report, April 1973.

———. *Decisions for Successful Living*. Salt Lake City: Deseret Book, 2009.

———. "Your Light to Be a Standard unto the Nations." *Ensign*, August 1973.

Levinson, Jon. *Sinai and Zion: An Entry into the Jewish Bible*. San Francisco: HarperSanFrancisco, 1985.

Lewis, C. S. *Christian Behaviour*. London: Macmillan, 1943.

———. *God in the Dock: Essays on Theology and Ethics*. Edited by Walter Hooper. Grand Rapids, MI: William B. Eerdmans, 2014.

———. *Mere Christianity*. New York: HarperOne, 2001.

———. *The Screwtape Letters*. Revised edition. New York: Macmillan, 1982.

———. "The Sermon and the Lunch." In *The Grand Miracle: And Other Selected Essays on Theology and Ethics from God in the Dock*. Edited by Walter Hooper. New York: Ballantine Books, 1970.

———. *The Weight of Glory*. New York: Touchstone, 1996.

Lincoln, Abraham. "First Inaugural Address of Abraham Lincoln." March 4, 1861. avalon.law.yale.edu/19th_century/lincoln1.asp.

Litwa, M. David. *Becoming Divine: An Introduction to Deification in Western Culture*. Eugene, OR: Cascade Books, 2013.

Macdonald, George. *The Miracles of our Lord*. London: Strahan & Co., 1870.

Madsen, Truman G. "The Suffering Servant." In *The Redeemer—Reflections on the Life and Teachings of Jesus the Christ*. Salt Lake City: Deseret Book, 2000.

Maxwell, Neal A. "Encircled in the Arms of His Love." *Ensign*, November 2002.

———. "Enduring Well." *Ensign*, May 1997.

———. "Insights from My Life." Brigham Young University devotional, October 26, 1976. speeches.byu.edu.

———. "Meek and Lowly." Brigham Young University devotional, October 21, 1986. speeches.byu.edu.

———. "Notwithstanding My Weakness." *Ensign*, November 1976.

———. "Patience." Brigham Young University devotional, November 27, 1979. speeches.byu.edu.

———. "Remember How Merciful the Lord Hath Been." *Ensign*, May 2004.

———. "Repentance." *Ensign*, November 1991.

McConkie, Bruce R. *A New Witness for the Articles of Faith*. Salt Lake City: Deseret Book, 1985.

———. *Mormon Doctrine*. 2nd edition. Salt Lake City: Bookcraft, 1966.

———. "Ten Keys to Understanding Isaiah." *Ensign*, October 1973.

McKay, David O. and Beverly Nichols. In David O. McKay, *Stepping Stones to an Abundant Life*. Salt Lake City: Deseret Book, 1971.

Bibliography

Miller, Adam S. *Grace Is Not God's Backup Plan: An Urgent Paraphrase of Paul's Letter to the Romans*. N.p., 2015.

Millet, Robert L. "This Is My Gospel." In *The Book of Mormon: 3 Nephi 9–30, This Is My Gospel*. Provo, UT: Religious Studies Center, 1993.

Monson, Thomas S. "Courage Counts." *Ensign*, November 1986.

Nelson, Russel M. "Closing Remarks." *Ensign*. November 2019.

———. "Drawing the Power of Jesus Christ into Our Lives." *Ensign*, May 2017.

———. "The Future of the Church: Preparing the World for the Savior's Second Coming." *Ensign*, April 2020.

———. In "Latter-day Saint Prophet, Wife and Apostle Share Insights of Global Ministry." October 30, 2018. newsroom.ChurchofJesusChrist.org.

Nibley, Hugh. *Approaching Zion*. Volume 9 in *The Collected Works of Hugh Nibley*. Salt Lake City: Deseret Book, 1989.

———. "On the Sacred and the Symbolic." In *Temples of the Ancient World: Ritual and Symbolism*. Edited by Donald W. Parry. Salt Lake City: Deseret Book, 1994.

Oaks, Dallin H. "Alternate Voices." *Ensign*, May 1989.

———. *The Lord's Way*. Salt Lake City: Deseret Book, 1991.

———. "Timing." Brigham Young University devotional, January 29, 2002. speeches.byu.edu.

Packer, Boyd. K. "Covenants," *Ensign*, November 1990.

———. "The Choice." *Ensign*, November 1980.

———. "Lehi's Dream and You." Brigham Young University devotional, January 16, 2007. speeches.byu.edu.

———. "Washed Clean." *Ensign*, May 1997.

Perry, L. Tom. "Becoming Self-Reliant." *Ensign*, November 1991.

Rector, Hartman, Jr. "How to Know If Revelation Is from the Lord." Brigham Young University devotional, January 6, 1976. speeches.byu.edu.

———. "You Shall Receive the Spirit." *Ensign*, November 1973.

Riddle, Chauncey C. "Prayer." *Ensign*, March 1975.

Rivkin, Ellis. *A Hidden Revolution*. Nashville: Abingdon, 1978.

Robbins, Lynn G. "Which Way Do You Face?" *Ensign*, November 2014.

Roberts, B. H. *A Comprehensive History of the Church*, 1:163.

Saint Anselm. In *Saint Anselm: Basic Answers*. 2nd edition. Translated by Sidney Norton Deane. LaSalle, IL: Open Court Publishing, 1962.

Scott, Richard G. "Trust in the Lord." *Ensign*, November 1995.

Smith, Joseph. In *History of the Church*, 5:336 (April 6, 1843).

———. In *Histories, Volume 1: Joseph Smith Histories, 1832–1844*.

Smith, Joseph F. *Gospel Doctrine*. Salt Lake City: Deseret Book, 1939.

Smith, Joseph Fielding. In Conference Report, October 1952.

Snow, Lorenzo. In *Collected Discourses Delivered by President Wilford Woodruff, His Two Counselors, the Twelve Apostles, and Others*. Compiled and edited by Brian H. Stuy. 5 volumes. Burbank, CA: B. H. S. Publishing, 1988, 4:55.

Stevenson, James. Editor. *A New Eusebius*. London: SPCK, 1957.

Talmage, James E. *Articles of Faith, Classics in Mormon Literature*. Salt Lake City: Deseret Book, 1984.

Bibliography

Tanner, Susan W. "Faith in Jesus Christ." *Religious Educator* 20, no. 2 (2019): 50.

Thompson, P. E. S. "The Yahwist Creation Story." *Vestus Testamentum* 21, no. 2 (April 2, 1971): 208.

Twain, Mark. *Mark Twain's Letters.* Volume 2. Arranged by Albert Bigelow Paine. New York: Harper & Brothers, 1917.

Uchtdorf, Dieter F. "The Infinite Power of Hope." *Ensign*, November 2008.

———. "Seeing Beyond the Leaf." *Religious Educator* 15, no. 3 (2014).

Van Orden, Bruce A. *Studies in Scripture, vol 6: Acts to Revelation.* Edited by Robert Millet. Salt Lake City: Deseret Book, 1987.

Vestor, Bertha Spafford. *Our Jerusalem, an American Family in the Holy City, 1881–1949.* Garden City, NY: Doubleday & Company, 1950.

Whitney, Orson F. "The Soul's Captain." *Improvement Era*, May 1926.

Wilcox, Brad. Personal notes from Education Week talk.

Wilcox, S. Michael. *Twice Blessed: The Beauty of Forgiving and Forgiveness.* Salt Lake City: Deseret Book, 2016.

Woodruff, Wilford. In Conference Report, April 1989, 29–30.

Young, Brigham. In *Journal of Discourses.*

Young, S. Dilworth. In Conference Report, April 1963.

About the Author

Marlow C. Hunter authored and published his first book, *The Education of Our Desires*, in 2018. He was born and raised in Wyoming, attended and graduated from Brigham Young University with a BA in mathematics, physics, and chemistry, and received a Secondary Education Teaching Certificate in 1971. He was awarded a Master of Business Administration, majoring in accounting and minoring in economics and finance, from the University of North Texas in 1974.

Seeing employment opportunities available with the large, international public accounting firms, he was hired by Arthur Anderson & Co. and completed the requirements to be licensed as a certified public accountant (CPA). He began his forty-five-year career in Dallas, Texas, where he worked with a variety of companies and organizations to fulfill their financial reporting responsibilities. After five-year stint with Anderson, he joined a colleague to form a CPA firm where he spent the next fifteen years.

In 1998, Marlow formed his own CPA firm with offices in Dallas and Chicago. He has given back to his profession by serving on several volunteer committees, including the Ethics Committee, which oversees CPA's compliance with the Code of Professional Conduct. His training in education became another way by which he serves the CPA community. In 1988, continuing professional education (CPE) became mandatory for CPAs in the USA. Over the last thirty years, Marlow has designed, developed, and written dozens of CPE seminars, as well as given hundreds of educational presentations, both in live and webcast formats, to thousands of CPAs.

Even more significant than his forty-five-year commitment to his profession is his dedication and devotion to The Church of Jesus Christ of Latter-day Saints. He has served as a counselor to three bishops, as a bishop, stake clerk, high councilor, temple ordinance worker, and adjunct institute instructor, as well as Gospel Doctrine Sunday school class and high priests quorum teacher. For the last sixteen years, Marlow has been conducting a stake-wide adult Gospel Education class.

Marlow lives in Chicago. He and his wife have six children and eighteen grandchildren. He can be reached at marlowcpa@yahoo.com. Other resources prepared by the author to assist in studying the gospel can be found at www.authormarlowchunter.com.

Also by Marlow Hunter

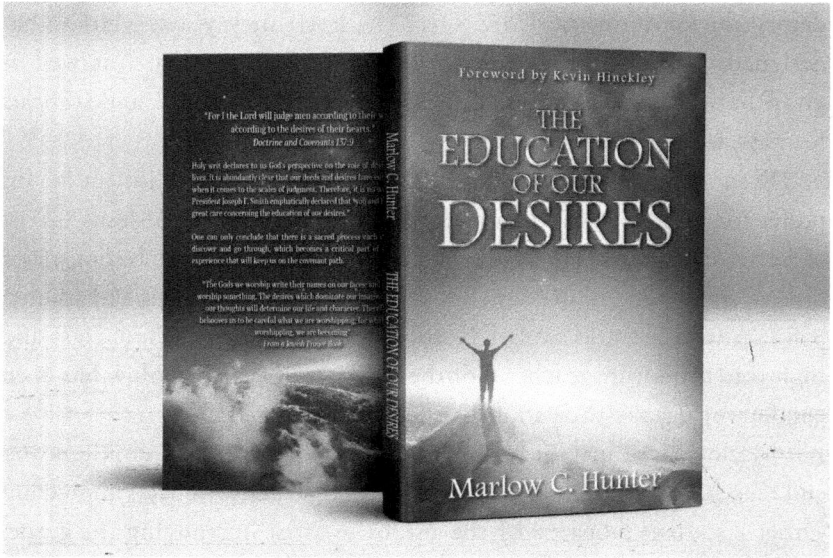

www.ingramcontent.com/pod-product-compliance
Lightning Source LLC
Chambersburg PA
CBHW072005090426
42740CB00011B/2097